GreatGROUPS
GOOD WORD SERIES

LEADER'S GUIDE

Gospel ON THE Go

15 SMALL GROUP STUDIES
IN THE BOOK OF MARK

GW00691665

DOUG SCHMIDT

David C. Cook Publishing Co.
Elgin, Illinois/Paris, Ontario

GREAT GROUPS
The Good Word Series
Gospel on the Go Leader's Guide
© 1994 David C. Cook Publishing Co.

Unless otherwise noted, Scripture quotations are from the Holy Bible, New International Version (NIV), © 1973, 1978, 1984 by International Bible Society. Used by permission of Zondervan Bible Publishers.

Published by David C. Cook Publishing Co.
850 North Grove Ave., Elgin, IL 60120
Cable address: DCCOOK
Series editor: Lorraine Triggs. Author: Doug Schmidt.
Designer: Jeff Sharpton, PAZ Design Group. Cover illustrator: Ken Cuffe.
Printed in U.S.A. ISBN: 0-7814-5130-2

TABLE OF Contents

Great Stuff about Great Groups!

Welcome to *Great Groups*—a new concept in youth ministry resources from David C. Cook.

Great Groups is a three-tiered series of studies created for high schoolers and young adults who are at various stages of spiritual development. The three tiers—designed to move young people from being casual about Christianity to becoming committed followers of Jesus Christ—look like this:

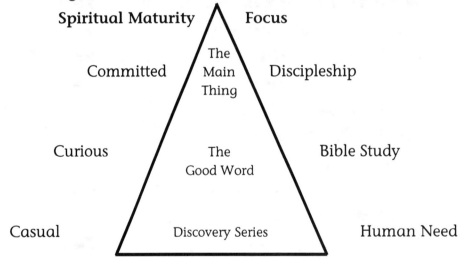

Spiritual Maturity   **Focus**

Committed — The Main Thing — Discipleship

Curious — The Good Word — Bible Study

Casual — Discovery Series — Human Need

***Great Groups* was created because:**

• Not all young people are at the same stage of spiritual development;

• Intentional ministry is needed to guide people toward greater spiritual commitment;

• Real life change is possible through studying the Bible individually *and* discussing it together in small groups;

• Many young people are ready to lead discussion groups, so these studies encourage peer leadership;

• No two small groups are the same, so these studies pay attention to group dynamics.

Discovery Series—entry-level studies for seekers and those who've grown up in the church, but who may not have a complete understanding of what it means to be a Christian. These studies help people discover who they are from God's perspective and the difference that can make in every area of their lives. The *Discovery Series* assumes group members have little or no Bible background. Minimal advance preparation needed.

The Good Word—inductive studies for those who are curious about what the Bible really says. These studies help young people develop lifelong Bible study skills that will challenge them to feed themselves from Scripture. *The Good Word* series assumes group members have little or some Bible background. Moderate advance preparation needed.

The Main Thing—discipleship studies for those who want to be followers of Jesus Christ. These studies will challenge group members to take their faith seriously. *The Main Thing* series assumes group members have some or extensive Bible background. Thorough advance preparation needed.

How to Use This Material

The Bible was never intended to be a book for scholars and specialists only. From the very beginning it was intended to be everybody's book, and that is what it continues to be.—F. F. Bruce (one of the world's greatest Bible scholars)

In case you were wondering . . .

Why a Small Group Bible Study?

As you go through the Bible study journal on your own, you'll dig into God's Word and make your own discoveries. In the small group, however, you'll not only have a chance to share what you've learned, but also to learn from others. Different people will make different discoveries about a passage, and this will increase each group member's understanding of Scripture.

The small group also acts as a check, as you always go back to something greater than yourselves, the Word of God. This Bible study isn't based on someone's opinion, but on the Bible.

Your group probably won't be made up of a bunch of Bible experts and specialists. But as F.F. Bruce said, the Bible is everybody's book and that's the beauty of studying it. God wants everyone to know what He says, and to put those truths into practice.

What Kind of Bible Study Is This?

The kind of Bible study you'll be doing is called an inductive study. Inductive means that you start with a Bible passage and learn to observe it directly—not what some book or person says about the passage. Each group member digs into the passage and discovers answers for himself or herself. As a leader of an inductive study, your role isn't to supply the "right" answers (phew), but to keep the study moving.

You'll also get some practice using different Bible study methods. You'll use the manuscript method as you study the Book of Mark.

If you looked in the Bible study journal, you probably noticed chunks of Bible text—with no verses, chapters, cross references, or footnotes. This was done intentionally to give you an idea of how the passage was originally written. As you go through the study, pretend that you're seeing it for the first time.

Another feature of the Bible study is the part you have in dividing the text into its natural parts. You underline, circle, and draw lines and arrows as you dig into the text and discover what it says and means. In your first meeting as a group, go over the basics of a manuscript study on pages 5 and 6 of the Bible study journal.

In other studies, you might do a character study or an overview study of a book, or outline a book, looking for its main themes. As a group, you'll have lots of practice in different methods, but the backbone of this study is inductive.

When you study the Bible, you follow the same rules of interpretation you'd use in interpreting any piece of literature. But first, a ground rule: The text is the authority. Stick to the passage under discussion and let it speak for itself.

Here are the three basic guidelines of interpretation:

1. What does the passage say? (Observation.) Answering this question involves the five Ws and one H questions of journalism.

• *Who* is writing? *Who* is the passage about? *Who* was the book originally written for (the audience)?

• *What* kind of writing is this? (Letter, poem, historical account, narrative, prophecy). *What* parts can we see? *What* are the author's tactics? *What* was the writer's train of thought in this passage? *What's* happening?

• *When* is all this happening? This does not mean just a date or year unless the text says so. It means at what point in Jesus' ministry. Or, after what and before what other events in the Bible. Or, at what time of day—whatever the text itself says about time.

• *Where* is the action taking place? What country, or at whose house, and what does the setting tell you?

• *Why?* Does one event or person cause something else to happen? What are the motives and feelings here? *Why* did the author write this? Is he persuading, reporting, worshiping, teaching?

• *How* does each of the parts relate to the whole portion of Scripture? *How* is the story or argument being told or arranged?

2. What does it mean? (Interpretation.) Once you've looked carefully at the text to find out what it actually says, you can look at its meaning. This is where most problems come in. Sometimes there are layers of meanings, but usually there is one basic meaning of the text, at least for the times in which it was written.

To discover the meaning of the text, ask questions such as this: how does the style affect our interpretation? Did the writer intend for this to be taken literally, or is it a story with a moral, such as the parables of Jesus? There are legitimate differences of interpretations for some passages, but discovering the writer's intent eliminates many, if not, most of the different meanings.

3. What does it mean to me? (Application.) Too often people jump right to this question the first time they read a passage. In fact, this is the last question you should answer. Only when the first two questions are answered can you legitimately ask what the passage means to you specifically, and to people in general.

The Holy Spirit is ultimately the interpreter of His Word to our hearts. You don't have to be a scholar to understand and "hear" God speaking to you through a verse or passage of Scripture. By jumping to this question without really understanding what the text actually says and what it means, you can come up with errors and weird interpretations.

Who Leads the Bible Study?

Anyone in the group can. These studies are designed for peer leadership. The leader doesn't have to be an expert. Each session has some leader's tips to help you in your role as leader. Basically, the leader's role in an inductive study is to ask questions and guide the group members into the text and dig out the meaning for themselves, rather than telling people what it means. You might want to rotate the leadership so everyone has a chance to lead. If some people don't want to lead a study, that's okay. Start off with someone who's led a Bible study before, go for a few weeks, and then hand off the leadership to someone else.

The leader's job is to facilitate discussion. Do not allow anyone—not even yourself—to monopolize the discussion. Try to draw out more reserved members, but don't force anyone to talk who doesn't want to. Give people time to think and don't be afraid of a little silence.

If someone comes up with an "off the wall" interpretation, ask something like, "Where do you see that meaning in the text?" Sometimes the group corrects itself. Someone might wonder about the comment and say what he or she sees in the verses. Or you could ask other people what they think—as long as they stick with the text too.

If someone brings up something that's off the subject of the text, say so, but offer to follow up on it later. Don't let the group get sidetracked into an argument. If there's a legitimate disagreement, let people express their points, and then say, "Let's move on; we can discuss this later," or even, "We probably have to agree to disagree about this, but let's continue with the study."

What Version of the Bible Should the Group Use?

The Scripture that's printed in the journal is in the New International Version. So obviously, that's the one we're recommending. It's a good idea for everyone to use the same version of the Bible. If your group needs the New International Version, contact the International Bible Society for inexpensive Bibles. You may want to have an alternate translation along for comparison purposes, but it avoids confusion when everyone is using the same version. Another value in using the same translation (and it would have to be the same edition) is that you can tell people what page to turn to for those who may have difficulty finding things in the Bible.

The Format

The study for the Book of Mark (and every other study in *The Good Word* series) breaks down into three five-week units. As a group, decide how many weeks you'll want to spend in the Book of Mark. Of course, we think it's a great idea to spend fifteen weeks, but do make a commitment of at least five weeks in the second Gospel.

Another group decision will need to be made about the actual length of time for the group study. You should always make sure to allow at least forty to forty-five minutes for the study itself and five to ten minutes for actual prayer at the end, not just sharing requests.

Here's the format of a meeting, plus suggested times.

1 Getting Started (15-20 minutes)

One of the most important parts of your time together. You can use this time to welcome new people to the group, encourage people to mingle, and get into the frame of mind to discuss the study for the week.

Housekeeping (3-5 minutes)

This is the place for announcements (for example, a change in the meeting location, a schedule change, or plans for a social activity outside of group time). Keep these short and sweet.

Icebreaker (5-10 minutes)

For the first couple of weeks, this section has fun, lighthearted activities. These activities will help people feel that the group is a safe place for sharing nonthreatening things. In later weeks of the study, the activity suggestions become more serious and lead to deeper sharing.

Opening (5 minutes)

The singing part is totally up to the group, but do open in prayer. If you absolutely panic about leading in prayer, take advantage of the prayer and litanies we provide. It's not unspiritual to read a prayer—but truly pray it. Don't just rattle it off.

2 Bible Study (40-60 minutes)

Focus (about 5 minutes)

This short transition is an activity or approach question that sets up the study and shows the relevance of it to people's lives. It answers questions such as, "Why is this study important to me? How will this relate to my life? How can it help me deal with the problems I'm facing?"

Usually the question or activity relates to something in the journals. And speaking of the Bible study journal, whenever you see this symbol, that's the cue that whatever follows—a question, paragraph, or activity—is from the Bible study journal. You'll need to use the journal and this book to lead the study.

Dig In (Observation and Interpretation) (20-30 minutes)

As far as inductive an Bible study goes, this section is the observation and interpretation steps. It's also the heart of the small group. Yes, there is the expectation that everyone will have completed the Bible study beforehand, so each person needs to bring his or her Bible study journal and Bible to the group each week. But this doesn't mean that if someone didn't finish the study, he or she can't participate. One of the best things about an inductive study is that a person can participate even without preparation. It might take him or her longer to contribute an observation or meaning, but the person can still contribute.

In this section, the goal of the leader is to move the group through the observation-interpretation process. Because the Bible study is a partially guided inductive study, the questions in the journal get the discussion going. There are suggested answers to the Bible study, but the emphasis is on the suggested. These are not the only answers that are right. Remember that the passage you're investigating is the authority, and a check on everyone's observations and interpretations. This section also has additional inductive questions for whoever is leading the study to ask the group.

Even though we've made a big deal about only using the Bible and not relying on other books, we still wanted to give the person leading the study some extra information. We put this information in a box called, "Inside Insights," and it might include definitions, an explanation of a custom, background about the audience, or a key idea.

Reflect and Respond (Application)
(5-10 minutes)

This section is the application step of the inductive process. It's here that you ask the "so what" questions. For example, "How did this study help me, challenge me, or relate to my life?" Or, "What have I learned and how have I changed as a result?" "What will I do as a result of this change?" Frequently, this will be a time for members to do something to show what they got out of the study.

3 Sharing and Prayer (15-20 minutes)

Here's the time where people may talk about what's going on in their lives, and what they would like prayer for. Begin with prayer needs that come out of the study, and then move to personal requests. Focus on personal needs, avoiding requests for someone's third cousin once-removed. You may want to keep the prayer time totally open-ended, or have some structure to it. Make sure that you spend some time in prayer, not just talking about yourselves until it's time to leave.

Off and Running

Overview

• Provide a general introduction to the Bible study group.

• Introduce inductive Bible study and the manuscript method.

• Begin the study of "Who Is Jesus?"

Scripture: Mark 1

1 Getting Started

Leader's Tip: Start on time even if everyone isn't there yet. People will come in late, but they'll catch on fast that the group is serious about its starting time. (And try to be as serious about ending on time too.)

Icebreaker

Here are a couple of ideas from *Incredible Meeting Makers: Mix It Up!* (© 1993 David C. Cook Publishing Co.). The first one is a good getting-to-know-you activity; the second idea is good practice for the observation step of an inductive Bible study.

As people arrive, give each person a sheet with these six different times listed:

6:17 A.M.	3:02 P.M.
8:41 A.M.	6:36 P.M.
12:12 P.M.	9:18 P.M.

For each time, ask group members: **What are you doing at this exact**

minute? After each person says what he or she is doing, ask people to raise their hands if they're doing the same thing. People may find they have more in common with others than they thought.

Here's the second icebreaker activity.

Have partners stand facing each other and talk about anything they want for one minute so they can get to know each other better. Don't mention anything about switching things. Next, ask partners to turn around and stand back to back so they can secretly change one thing about their appearance. They could untuck a shirt, roll up sleeves, take off a watch, take off glasses, switch rings around, change hairstyle, untie (or tie) a shoe, etc. After all adjustments are made, have partners face each other again and try to determine what has changed. Some will probably be unsuccessful. Play additional rounds and see if people get more perceptive. Talk about how we miss so much in our lives because we are not aware of all that goes on around us.

Housekeeping (Usually you'll take care of business first, but today this section is a bit longer.)

Make the break from any goofiness (and allow for the inevitable late-comer) by giving any announcements after the icebreaker activity and before getting serious. Keep it short. This week, you'll want to nail down the meeting time of the small group. Once you decide when, where, how often, and how long you'll meet, decide how you'll handle leadership. (See page 8 for suggestions.)

Because this is the first meeting, introduce the group to the series by saying something like this: **There are a lot of wrong assumptions about the Bible. Partly because people have no idea what it says, partly because people misinterpret what it does say.**

In this group, we're going to investigate what the Bible has to say for itself. We're not going to be dependent on what a pastor, teacher, or theological book says *about* the Bible, but seek to examine what the Bible says directly.

Hand out copies of the Bible study journals and explain how to use them.

This Bible study isn't a question-and-answer, fill-in-the-blanks study. Your journal is designed to help you dig into a Bible passage, make your own observations, discover the meaning of the passage, and then figure out

what the passage means to you. In the group, we'll look at the same passage and have a chance to share our discoveries, ask questions, and learn from each other.

At the end of each week, there's a section called "Personal Prayer." (Ask the group to flip to that section.) **The idea here is to think about what you've been studying, and then express your thoughts and feelings to God in writing.** There's usually a sentence starter or something else to help you. One advantage to writing out your prayers is that you'll be able to look back and see how God has been at work in your life.

Turn back to the regular Bible study section. Today, we'll do Week 1 together. For the next time, prepare Week 2. The Bible study should be done before the next group meeting. It probably can be done in about thirty minutes. But you might want to spread it out over a couple of days. Even when you don't finish the study ahead of time, come to the group anyhow. You can still make a contribution.

Opening

If someone in the group plays an instrument, ask if he or she would be willing to lead singing each week. You don't have to sing at all, but there'll be song suggestions that go along with the theme. Most of the songs can be found in songbooks available in Christian bookstores.

Here's a prayer you may want to use as you begin this study in the Gospel of Mark:

God, as we begin this study in the Gospel of Mark, help us have open minds to discover what Your Word says about Jesus, and ourselves. I pray that this small group becomes a place where we can talk honestly and encourage each other. Thank You for the opportunity to study Your Word. In Jesus' name. Amen.

2 Bible Study

Focus

Read the introduction to this unit's study, "Zoom In on Jesus' life" (page 7 in the Bible study journal), and then discuss the two questions in the journal. (They're on page 9 in the journal.)

 Before jumping into this study, list some ways people describe Jesus. How would you describe Jesus? (For example, He was a great teacher.)

 Suppose the descriptions on your list were all you knew about Jesus. Based on these descriptions, what kind of person would you think Jesus was?

As a group, talk about the different ways people (yourselves included) describe Jesus, and what kind of conclusions you could make about Jesus. After a few minutes, explain that this study in the Gospel of Mark is all about Jesus. In fact, you're going to zoom in on Jesus' life while He was on earth, and find out about His teachings, His relationships, and His character.

Say something such as this: **Let's look at Jesus' question, "Who do you say I am?" as an invitation to get to know Him better and find out who He really is.**

Dig In

Before doing the actual study, have everyone turn to the section, "How to Do This Bible Study" (page 5 of the Bible study journal). Make sure everyone understands the basics of the manuscript method of inductive Bible study. First, point out the reprint of Mark 1 on pages 9-11. Most people should notice that the Bible passage doesn't have any verses marked.

Explain: **Pretend that you're seeing this for the first time. Since the author didn't write in verses, his manuscript isn't divided up into neat little segments. Part of the manuscript method involves dividing the chapter into its natural parts, or scenes.**

We're going to mark up this passage, highlight important words, and seek to discover what it says—without relying on other books about the passage.

Don't worry about the color code system for now; just get used to marking up the text. As the group leader for this meeting, you'll find more information about the rules of interpretation on page 7 of this book.

Say: **By doing this study as a group, we'll all get some practice in using the manuscript method of Bible study.**

Ask everyone to turn to page 9 in the journal and begin reading Mark 1 from there. When people have finished, they may move on to the next two questions. Give everyone about ten minutes to read and mark up the chapter.

1. Reread Mark 1 and decide what kind of writing it is (for example, first person or third person, narrative, a story, or a letter). Make other observations about the kind of writing you see here (for example, active or passive voice, its style, and choice of words). What's the author's purpose? (Did Mark state his purpose up front?)

2. Divide the text into natural parts or sections in green or the color of your choice. (Hint: Look for a change in scenes, characters, places, and actions.) Draw lines between the different sections. You can mark up the Scripture right here in your journal.

Call the group back together, and ask different people to report their observations about the kind of writing and the author's purpose. (Here are some possible answers: the writing is third person narrative. It possibly could be biographical because it focuses on one main person, Jesus. Mark jumps from incident to incident. One purpose for this chapter is stated in verse one: to tell about "the beginning of the gospel about Jesus Christ, the Son of God.")

Leader's Tip: Encourage people to get in the habit of supporting their answers from the Bible passage under investigation. As long as an answer can be supported by the text, it's legitimate.

Next, compare the different ways group members divided the chapter. Ask: **Why did you choose to divide it that way?**

Break for another ten minutes or so to complete the instructions in question three. The sentence summaries should be short; and the titles can be funny, creative, or matter-of-fact. When time is up, group members may share their summaries and titles.

Ask: **Are you okay with the way you divided the chapter?** If anyone suggests a change, ask the person to explain his or her reasons why—again, supported by what's there in Mark 1.

Once you've finished with the section summaries, give group members ten minutes to complete questions four and five. If they want to, people may draw lines to connect the related ideas, or circle the repeated words. Really mark up the text in the Bible study journal.

As far as the observations go, get your group members to look at the details in the passage. The who, what, where, when, why, and how questions will help them with their observations.

Come back together and report on your findings. Keep in mind that you're still at the observation step of the Bible study process, so be careful not to read things into the passage that aren't there.

Say: **Describe some of the emotions people probably felt, including Jesus' emotions.** Again, group members should only describe what's there in the passage. Get them to look at the way people said things, the verbs Mark chose to use, as well as directly stated emotions. (For example, "Filled with compassion, Jesus reached out and touched the man. . . .")

Leader's Tip: When you ask one of the discussion questions, give people time to think of their answers. Don't be afraid of a little silence. If no one says anything, rephrase the question or come back to it later. Never answer your own questions.

With these next questions, you'll move into the interpretation step of the Bible study.

Ask: **What do you think is significant about the words and phrases that are related or repeated? What do you think Mark wanted to communicate?** (For example, by using phrases such as "without delay," "as soon as," and "immediately," Mark communicated a sense of urgency and action.)

Again, always go back to the text. (We can't overstate this!) If someone gives an obviously off-base answer, someone in the group may get things back on track, or ask the person where he or she got that idea from the text.

 Finally, ask question six from the Bible study journal.

To help people come up with the meaning, encourage them to look at the chapter as a whole, not at some isolated verse or incident. Here are some suggested meanings from Mark 1: Repentance and belief are vital to the kingdom of God. Jesus came to preach and proclaim the good news of God. Jesus is the Son of God, who performed miracles and amazed people with His power and authority.

And one last set of questions to discuss: **Did you see anything in this**

INSIDE INSIGHTS

■ Mark uses the word "immediately" forty-two times, and uses the conjunction "and" four hundred times to keep the story moving. Even though its the shortest of the four Gospels, Mark records more miracles than in the other gospels. The emphasis is more on what Jesus did than on what He said.

■ In Mark 1:1, we're introduced to Jesus as the Son of God. Later on, some Roman Caesars actually used this same title for themselves.

■ Mark, like the Gospel of John, doesn't have a Christmas story. Instead Mark begins with the ministry of John the Baptist. John's practice of baptizing people who came to him in repentance earned him the name of "the Baptist" or "Baptizer." Baptism wasn't a new idea to John's audience. They knew of baptism for Gentile converts to Judaism, but had never heard that descendants of Abraham (the Jews) needed to repent and be baptized too.

chapter that you haven't seen before? Anything that was new to you? Why do you think it's important to see Jesus in these different situations and settings?

This is a good place for people to ask any questions they might have about Mark 1.

As a group, investigate the chapter for the answers.

Reflect and Respond

Give group members a couple of minutes to express their views of Jesus as He's pictured in Mark 1. Talk about this question: **Imagine that you're with Simon, Andrew, James, and John. What do you think was going through their minds when Jesus said to follow Him? What would be going through your mind? What would be different for you if you followed Jesus? What would be exciting? What would be hard?**

When you've finished, have everyone complete the prayer in the Personal Prayer section of the Bible study journal. If you feel it's appropriate, say something such as this: **No matter how we described our relationships with Jesus, it's a starting point in answering Jesus' question, "Who do you say I am?"**

3 Sharing and Prayer

As you end your first meeting, talk about what's going on in your lives and pray for one another. Before people leave, remind them to take time during the week to dig into Mark 2.

Health-Care Reform

Overview

• To explain why Jesus came for sinners, and not for the so-called righteous people.

• To show that a relationship with Jesus involves a radically different lifestyle.

Scripture: Mark 2

1 Getting Started

Housekeeping

Welcome everyone to the group, and check to see if everyone has a journal and a Bible. You might want to bring some extra Bibles in case someone needs one. If you have any new group members, go over the purpose of these Bible studies in the Gospel of Mark (to discover who Jesus is) and explain the kind of Bible study it is (inductive). Make any necessary announcements, then get started.

Icebreaker

Hold a sick joke contest. Group members may tell the worst puns or jokes they know, but they have to be kept clean—no obscene, off-color, or racist jokes. When someone has thought of a joke, he or she should stand up and tell it. The rest of the group votes on the joke: one groan if it's so-so, two groans if it's semi-sick, three groans if it's fairly sick, and four groans if it's simply awful.

Here are two examples of jokes.

• Why shouldn't you iron your four-leaf clover? Because you don't want to press your luck. (Our personal favorite.)

• If they would have had cameras in old Russia, Peter the Great would have been a movie tsar.

To get people in the mood for the study, ask: **Unfortunately, there are a lot of sick things in life that we can't laugh at. In your opinion, what's the worst "sickness" or problem in the world?**

Explain that while on earth, Jesus exposed the root cause for a lot of the world's illness and offered the only cure as well.

 ## Opening

A good song to open with is the third verse of the hymn, "O for a Thousand Tongues to Sing." Here are the words to that verse; either sing it together, or ask someone to read the words aloud to the group.

He speaks and listening to his voice
New life the dead receive
The mournful broken hearts rejoice
The humble poor believe
Hear him you deaf, you voiceless ones,
Your loosened tongues employ
You blind behold your Savior come
And leap you lame for joy!

by Charles Wesley/James Ward, © 1984. Music by Anno Domini Music.

Here's a prayer to use or adapt for this week's study:

Jesus, it's easy to recognize how sick and sinful the world is, but it's not as easy to admit that we're sinful and sick too. As we discover more about You, help us understand why You came to earth and how You offer the only remedy for sin. In Your name. Amen.

 Bible Study

Focus

Go around the group and share your cure-alls for the world. Get people to talk about how they would administer their cures, and why the cures would be effective. If someone has suggested Jesus as the cure-all for the world, ask the person to explain what exactly Jesus can cure and how.

Ask: **If you had one get-well message for the world, what would it be?** Encourage group members to imitate the typical get-well cards; the messages could be humorous, inspirational, or poetic.

Even if people have suggested Jesus as the cure-all for the world, say something like this: **We're going to look at Jesus' cure-all for the world and how He administered it. The only problem was that the most religious people of Jesus' day had trouble swallowing the pill.**

Leader's Tip: Instead of just talking about get-well messages, have group members actually make the cards. You'll need to bring a package of construction paper and markers or crayons to the small group, but that's all the supplies you'll need. When people have finished, pass the cards around the group or show them one at a time.

Dig In

Ask group members to explain how they divided Mark 2 into sections as well as read their section summaries and titles. The discussion questions go through these major sections one at a time: the healing of the paralytic, the call of Levi, the question about fasting and the wineskins, and the sabbath-day dilemma.

Most people probably marked the healing of the paralytic as the first section, but don't worry if people have different sections marked off—the discussion probably will go just fine.

Based on the observations members made about the passage (question four, page 18 of the Bible study journal), discuss these questions about the healing of the paralytic.

Look at this section again, and let's describe as many details as we can about this story. (For example, Capernaum was home to Jesus; the whole house and even outside was crammed with people; the four friends had to dig through the roof, Jesus knew in His spirit what the Pharisees were thinking, and so on.)

When the four men lowered the mat and the paralyzed man down to Jesus, He saw their faith. Did you see it? How did these men show their faith?

Who would you say was the dominating presence in the house, and why?

As it's been said before, as long as a person can support his or her response from the Bible text, it's legitimate. Don't worry about differences of opinions. For example, Jesus is the obvious dominant presence. The Pharisees dominated the scene too, especially when they challenged Jesus' authority to forgive sins (see Mark 2:6, 7).

Why do you think Jesus didn't heal the man first then forgive his sins?

This next batch of questions focus on the call of Levi, aka Matthew. Plan to use the information about tax collectors and Matthew from Inside Insights to fill in some background details for the group.

What do you think the expression "tax collectors and 'sinners' " means?

As group members talk about their observations, explain the position of tax collectors in Jesus' day (see Inside Insights). Also explain that sinners were notoriously evil people, who didn't follow the Pharisees' interpretation of the law. The expression was commonly used of tax collectors, adulterers, robbers, and the like. (This information came from the note on Mark 2:15 in the NIV Study Bible.)

Who were the healthy and righteous, and who were the sick and sinners Jesus described?

The Pharisees wanted to know why Jesus ate with tax collectors and sinners. What do you think their question implied about Jesus?

One implication might be that they thought Jesus was a sinner too, since He ate with sinners.

The following questions focus on the question about fasting and the sabbath.

Ask: **What do you think the illustrations about the bridegroom, the garment, and the wineskins mean?**

Get group members to talk about the contrast between feasting at a wedding and fasting. Weddings are joyous occasions for celebration, and fasting is usually associated with sorrow. Use the information about wineskins from Inside Insights to help group members understand this illustration.

If people have trouble with these illustrations, explain that the Pharisees had turned religion into a joyless, somber duty. Jesus offered a relationship that was joyous, and so radical that it couldn't contain the old religious establishment—just as brittle, old wineskins couldn't contain the new wine.

 From what you discovered about the characters' motives (question six in the Bible study journal), why do you think the Pharisees followed Jesus around?

How did Jesus handle these confrontations with the Pharisees?

As far as you can tell, what were the Pharisees concerned about? What was Jesus concerned about?

Skim Mark 2 and choose the key passage that sums up the meaning.

Get group members to choose a key passage based on what they wrote down for question nine in their Bible study journals. Most likely, someone in the group will pick Mark 2:17. If no one does, do us a favor, and you pick it!

Reflect and Respond

Move into this section by asking someone to read Mark 2:17, and then have people put this verse in their own words. For example: "It isn't the healthy who need a doctor, but the sick. I haven't come for self-righteous people, but for people who know they're sinners and need help."

Ask: **What did you discover about Jesus, and having a relationship with Him?**

Here are some discoveries about Jesus: He healed people—both physically and spiritually; He has the power to forgive sins; He associated with the outcasts

INSIDE INSIGHTS

■ Do you know why the men could dig through the roof (see Mark 2:4)? Because the typical roof was made of timbers laid about two or three feet apart; then sticks were laid close to each other, making the basic roof. Reeds, tree branches, and thistles were laid across this, and then packed down with about a foot of dirt.

■ A tax collector had to hand over an assessed figure at the end of the year, but could keep whatever he gathered beyond that. You could imagine the potential for extortion. A tax collector could stop anyone on the road, make the person unpack his bundles, and then charge just about anything they wanted as a tax on the items.

■ Levi son of Alphaeus is Matthew, the tax collector. (Check out Matthew 9:9; 10:3.) Matthew made his situation worse, because he was a Jew who worked for the Roman government. He probably was tagged Matthew by Jesus, and his new name means "gift of God." There's a bit of divine irony that the rip-off artist would become a gift of God to his people.

■ Goatskins were used to hold wine. As the fresh grape juice fermented, the wine would expand, and the new wineskin would stretch. Old wineskins, however, were brittle and inflexible, and wouldn't expand with the new wine.

and sinners of His day, not with the religious establishment; He confronted His opponents.

Say something like this: **As far as our relationship with Jesus goes, He came to heal us from our sin. He comes to people who realize their need for Him. And He gives sinners a new life that can't be contained in old religious structures or old lives.**

To close, read the following quote to group members: **"The first link between my soul and Christ is not my goodness, but my badness; not my merit, but my misery; not my standing, but my falling; not my riches, but my need."**

Ask group members to think about their relationship with Jesus. Suggest that people reread what they wrote in the Personal Prayer section of their journals. Ask: **Is what you wrote still fairly accurate of how you feel about your relationship with the Lord? Do you want to change anything?**

We're not going to ask you to "give an invitation," but just in case someone wants to know how to have this relationship with Jesus, here's an explanation of salvation. It would be awesome for you to be involved in someone's decision to come to Christ.

• God wants everyone to enjoy the best life possible. He wants all of us to have a full life and experience His love (Jeremiah 31:3).

• But everybody has rebelled against God and sinned. Romans 3:23 says, "For all have sinned and fall short of the glory of God."

• Sin separates us forever from God. And it gets worse: we deserve to pay a penalty because we sinned (Romans 6:23).

• Only God could solve the problem, and He did! He loved us so much that He sent His Son, Jesus, to die, paying the penalty we deserved (John 3:16, 17).

• You aren't forced to accept God's solution. To apply Jesus' payment for sin to your life, you must personally commit yourself in belief to Him.

• You can have forgiveness. If you declare openly that Jesus died for your sins and believe that God raised Him from the death, God has promised you eternal life (Romans 10:9; I Corinthians 15:3, 4; I John 5:11). As you study the Bible and talk with God through prayer, you will grow closer to Him and enjoy the full life He intended (John 10:10).

3 Sharing and Prayer

In closing, give group members a chance to talk about what's going on in their lives and what they would like the group to pray about. As the weeks go by, you'll also want to report on answers to prayers and the different ways God is working in all of your lives.

Before people start to leave, remind them to complete Week 3 for the next small group meeting.

Out of His Mind

WEEK 3

Overview

• To look at the different opinions people had about Jesus while He was on earth.

• To realize that everyone has to make a choice about who Jesus is, and about joining His spiritual family.

Scripture: Mark 3

1 Getting Started

Housekeeping

It's possible that people are still joining the group. If so, welcome any new group members, go over the purpose of these Bible studies in the Gospel of Mark (to discover who Jesus is) and explain the kind of Bible study it is (inductive). Make any necessary announcements, then get started.

Icebreaker

Give group members a few minutes to think of some outrageous things that have happened to them. Explain that each person will get a chance to tell his or her story, and the object of the storytelling is to tell the tallest tale possible. In other words, try to top each other's stories.

Create a panel of "judges," who will rank each story on a scale of one to ten, with ten being the top score. To show his or her score, each judge holds up the appropriate number of fingers—10 fingers, 8.5 fingers, 4.75, and so on. Have the judges declare the top teller of tall tales, applaud the winner, and move on to the more serious stuff.

Say something like this: **As Jesus' fame grew, stories about Him probably were making the rounds. But none of the stories could ever top who Jesus really was and why He came to earth.**

Opening

The Book of Psalms is full of songs and praises about God's mighty works and wonders to His people, the Israelites. Psalm 136 is one of these psalms. It's a liturgy of praise for all God has done for His people. Read this psalm responsively, with group members repeating the refrain, "His love endures forever."

When you've finished reading the psalm, here's a prayer to use or adapt for this study:

God, thank You that Your love endures forever. Thank You for giving us Your Son, Jesus. As we discover more about Jesus, help us also to discover what it means to become part of Your family and follow You. In Jesus' name. Amen.

3 Bible Study

Focus

Ask group members to describe some of their family members—naturally, in the kindest, most loving ways. For example, they could explain family nicknames or things family members are known for (like the family firebug or the family animal lover). You might want to set some limits to the descriptions, such as no negative or derogatory descriptions. Also, make sure group members know they don't have to share anything if they don't want to.

Say: **Think about Jesus' family. How do you think they would describe Him? What do you think the neighbors would say about Jesus?** In Luke's gospel, the hometown folks were amazed at Him. To them, Jesus was just the carpenter Joseph's son. They didn't believe He was the Messiah.

Leader's Tip: Whenever you talk about families, remember that there are no perfect families. Someone in the group may be going through a family crisis or another person might feel totally cut off from his or her family. Because of this, keep activities like the one in Focus on the light side of things.

Dig In

Begin with group members sharing any questions they had about Mark 3 as well as anything that stood out to them in this chapter (see question two in the Bible study journal). Encourage group members to help each other look for answers, based on their observations and interpretations of the text.

Say something like this: **Let's take a closer look at Jesus' interchange with the Pharisees about the sabbath. What do you think was Jesus' point about the sabbath?** (By healing the man, Jesus demonstrated that He was ultimately in control of the sabbath. God never had intended the sabbath to be reduced to a bunch of rules and regulations. Instead the sabbath was for people's benefit—a chance to be restored physically, mentally, and spiritually.)

Is there anything ironic about this section? As a group, contrast Jesus' attitude about the sabbath—doing good and saving life—with the Pharisees' reaction to Jesus—plotting to kill Him. And these were the religious leaders of the day. No wonder Jesus blasted them.

What kind of pressure do you think this confrontation with the Pharisees put on Jesus?

Jesus seems to be going to extremes. One minute He's facing off with people who want to kill Him; the next minute He's surrounded by a mob of people who can't get enough of Him. How do you think the crowd added to the pressure?

Get group members to describe the scene of the crowd moving in on Jesus, begging to be healed, touching Him. Point out another source of pressure—the evil spirits, who kept crying out, "You are the Son of God." (See Mark 3:11.)

Some group members may have placed a question mark next to this portion of Scripture. If so, you may want to add this: The demons and evil spirits called out, "You are the Son of God," in an attempt to make Jesus powerless.

There was an ancient belief that the knowledge of the precise name or quality of a person meant that you would have control over him or her. That might be the reason Jesus didn't want them to speak. Also, the evil spirits recognized who Jesus was, but didn't believe in Him, so they weren't exactly the proper channel to disclose Jesus' identity.

Jesus felt all this pressure as a man. How did Jesus handle this pressure?

Skim the rest of the chapter and come up with ways Jesus handled the pressure. Here are a couple of things we found: Jesus eventually got away from the crowd, and He called other people to share in His ministry (the apostles).

What do you think that means for us when we feel pressure?

 Take a couple of minutes to talk about the main characters in this chapter, especially their relationship to Jesus (question three in the journal, page 26). Pay attention to the details of this section. For example, Jesus couldn't even eat in peace because of the crowd.

Why do you think Jesus' family came down to take charge of Him? Perhaps they were worried about Him; or maybe they thought Jesus had gone just a little too far.

Jesus' family didn't know what to think of Him, and the teachers of the law thought He was possessed by Beelzebub. What do you think was the point of Jesus' parable?

Here's one possible answer. If Jesus was possessed by Beelzebub, why would He want to drive out evil spirits? That would be self-defeating. Only someone stronger than Satan, stronger than the evil spirits can overpower Satan—and that's exactly what Jesus proved when He freed people from the evil spirits.

What does this tell you about Jesus?

And now you get to the verses that talk about the "unpardonable sin." First of all, you really don't want to get into any arguments or tangents about what the unpardonable sin is or isn't.

Here's some basic information from R. Kent Hughes in his commentary on the Gospel of Mark (*Mark, Jesus, Servant and Savior,* published by Crossway Books) to help you deal with the topic, if it comes up. From the context of Matthew

12:31 and of Mark 3:28-30, the Pharisees and the teachers of the law were attributing Christ's miracles done in the power of the Holy Spirit, and which authenticated His divine nature, to Satan. The unpardonable sin isn't cursing the Holy Spirit or taking the Lord's name in vain. It's not adultery or sexual perversion. And it's not even murder or genocide. Again, from the context, it involves an ongoing, continual rejection of the witness of the Holy Spirit to Jesus' divinity and His saviorship. If a person cares at all about what he or she is doing, then there's hope for forgiveness.

How do you think Jesus' family reacted to His question, "Who are my mother and my brothers?"

As you talk about Jesus' family, have group members share their responses from question eight in the journal.

From Jesus' answer, what do you discover about being a part of Jesus' family—His spiritual family that is?

Reflect and Respond

Everyone—the Pharisees, the crowd, the evil spirits, and the family—had an opinion about Jesus.

If you had been in that crowd, what would your opinion have been? (See question nine, page 27 in the journal.)

Jesus didn't leave much room for people to ignore Him or dismiss Him as a good moral teacher. As C. S. Lewis, a British writer, wrote: "A man who was merely a man and said the sort of things Jesus said wouldn't be a great moral teacher. He'd either be a lunatic—on a level with the man who says he's a poached egg—or else he'd be the Devil of Hell. You must make your choice."

Encourage group members to think seriously about their choice to follow Jesus. It's the most important decision they'll ever make, and one they won't ever regret.

3 Sharing and Prayer

■ This is the case of politics making strange bedfellows. The Pharisees were nationalistic and hated the Roman rule, and the Herodians were influential Jews who supported the Roman rule of the Herods. Both were afraid of Jesus' influence and sway over the crowd, so they ganged up against Him. The next time you see the plotting of the Pharisees and the Herodians is on Tuesday of Passion Week (Mark 12:13).

■ Here are some facts about the apostles. The name "Sons of Thunder" probably described James's and John's dispositions. Thaddaeus was apparently the same as "Judas son of James" (see Luke 6:16). Simon the Zealot was either a description of his religious zeal or a reference to Simon's membership in the party of the Zealots—a revolutionary group of Jews violently opposed to Roman rule. All the lists of the apostles begin with Simon Peter and end with Judas Iscariot.

■ Beelzebub is the prince of demons, and eventually the name came to be used of Satan.

■ Who were the other members of Jesus' earthly family? Mark 6:3 names four brothers: James, Joseph, Judas, and Simon; and mentions some sisters. Apparently Joseph, His earthly father, died before Jesus began His public ministry.

As you close, give group members a chance to talk about what's going on in their lives and what they would like the group to pray about. If you've been praying about some particular requests, this might be a good time to ask for an update.

Before people start to leave, remind them to complete Week 4 for the next small group meeting.

Storyteller

Overview

• To examine Jesus' parables in Mark 4.

• To realize that the more open a person is to God's truth the more understanding he or she will have of it.

Scripture: Mark 4

1 Getting Started

Housekeeping

Have you been taking turns leading the group? If so, this might be a good time to remind leaders about which weeks they're leading the group, and if needed, swap weeks. Make any necessary announcements, then get started.

Icebreaker

Once people have settled in, announce that they're going to get a chance to rewrite the story lines of well-known children's stories or nursery rhymes. Here's the catch: The rewrites have to be topics for a talk show. For example, "Have you ever felt like no one could ever put your life back together? Our guest will talk about how one fall ruined him, and not even government officials could help." (That's "Humpty, Dumpty.")

Group members could do this in pairs or small teams, and take turns guessing the story or nursery rhyme.

When you've finished, say something like this: **Jesus told stories to make a point and communicate spiritual truths. The Bible calls these stories "parables."**

 # Opening

If the group feels like singing, you might want to sing, "Righteousness, Peace, Joy." Here are words to that song.

Righteousness, peace, joy in the Holy Ghost
Righteousness, peace, joy in the Holy Ghost
That's the kingdom of God
(repeat)

Don't you wanna be a part of the kingdom,
Don't you wanna be a part of the kingdom,
Don't you wanna be a part of the kingdom,
Come on, everybody
(repeat)

There's joy in the kingdom,
So much joy in the kingdom,
There's joy in the kingdom,
Come on, everybody

© 1988 Integrity's Hosanna c/o Intergrity Music

Here's a prayer you can use or adapt for this study:

Thank You, God, that You want us to be a part of Your kingdom, a part of Your family. As we investigate Mark 4, give us eyes to see and ears to ear Your truth from Your Word. In Jesus' name. Amen.

 Bible Study

Focus

Ask group members how they would complete this sentence and why: **The kind of book that best describes my life right now is** _____, **because** _____. To get people in the groove, you could suggest these kinds of books: a romance novel, a mystery, or a sci-fi book.

Move in to the Bible study with this comment: **The Book of Mark tells the story of Jesus. Jesus not only performed miracles but He also taught spiritual truths—truths that people weren't always ready to hear or understand.**

Dig In

Ask group members to finish this sentence: **A parable is. . . .** Some of your more literary group members might know what a parable is. There's a definition in Inside Insights.

With group members using their summaries and observations they've made about Mark 4, spend the bulk of your time taking apart the parables and discussing the meanings.

Here's a reprint of the chart from question four in the Bible study journal, with some sample answers filled in for the first parable in Mark 4. Use the chart for each parable in Mark 4. It's a lot of work, but it will help group members understand the meaning of each parable.

Title	Different images	The Action/Results	Summary
Parable of the Sower	farmer, seeds, rocky, shallow soil, seed among thorns, seed in good soil	farmer planted seed seed that fell on the path was eaten by birds seed sown in rocky, shallow soil withered seed sown among thorns grew but was choked by thorns seed sown in good soil grew and produced a crop	Depending on where the farmer sowed the seed made a difference in whether or not the seed would grow and produce a crop.

When you've finished, discuss the meanings of the parables (refer to questions five and six, page 33 in the journal). Inside Insights helps explain those oh-so ordinary things in Jesus' days that may not be so commonplace today. Fortunately, Jesus explained the meaning of the parable of the sower.

Ask: **In two of the parables about the seed planting, what's the seed?**

(The seed is the word of God. In this case, the word of God that Jesus has been teaching.)

How are these two parables different? In the parable of the sower, the emphasis is on the soil, or on the person's receptivity to the Word. In the parable of the growing seed the emphasis is on the seed itself, or the power of the Gospel and God's truth.

What do these parables tell you about the Word of God and His kingdom?

What do you think is our role when we hear God's truth? How should we respond?

We either can choose to accept the truth, and more truth will be given to us, or we can reject God's truth or not respond to it, and never benefit from it. That's the idea of the phrase, "With the measure you use, it will be measured to you" phrase in Mark 4:24.

Why do you think Jesus compared the kingdom of God to a mustard seed? This would be a good time to share the information about the mustard seed from Inside Insights. Like that tiny seed, the kingdom of God got a pretty insignificant start on earth with a baby born in a stable. When Jesus begins His ministry, He chooses a group of twelve insignificant disciples to help share His ministry. And as Jesus taught these parables, the religious leaders were already plotting His death. Things really didn't get off to a bang.

Why do you think Jesus just didn't say exactly what He meant?

Encourage group members to answer this base on the parables. If anyone brings up Mark 4:10-12, check out the comments on this passage in Inside Insights. This isn't the easiest passage to understand or accept. It has been called one of Jesus' "hard sayings."

Take another look at the parable of the sower in the first part of the chapter.

 Which soil did you say best described you and why? (See question seven, page 33 in the Bible study journal.)

As you talk about this question, get people to describe attitudes today that would fit the types of soil. For example, a person who feels he or she is too intelligent or sophisticated for God would fit the hard, shallow soil.

 Switch gears and talk about the storm (the last part of Mark 4). First, get group members to describe the storm, based on their observations and discoveries in question eight of the journal.

Ask: **What do you think motivated the disciples to wake up Jesus—faith or fear?**

Do you think the disciples had an appropriate reaction to what Jesus had just done? Why or why not?

As the group discusses this question, get people to explain how they would have answered the disciples' question—rhetorical though it may be.

Reflect and Respond

Say something like this: **Actually, the only logical answer to the disciples' question is that Jesus is the Son of God. All He had to do was speak two words, and the wind and waves obeyed Him and the storm died down. If Jesus can control creation like that, what does that mean for you and your personal storms?**

Give people an opportunity to talk about some of their fears or situations where they needed to trust Jesus more (see the Personal Prayer page in the journal). You or another group leader might want to share something first.

Next, go around the group and have members complete this open-ended sentence: **I can trust Jesus during my personal storms, because. . . .** As always, let people know they may pass if they choose to.

3 Sharing and Prayer

Use the sentence completions from Reflect and Respond to begin your prayer time; then pray for each other this way: If someone has a prayer request, he or she may pray aloud for it, and then others in the group can pick up on the request and pray for it too.

Before people depart, remind them to complete Week 5 for the next small group meeting.

INSIDE INSIGHTS

■ A parable is usually a story out of ordinary life used to illustrate a spiritual or moral truth. It teaches people something they didn't know by comparing it to something they do know. The truth can be communicated by similes, comparisons, analogies, or sayings. A parable typically has one main point and not every detail of the story is significant.

■ There were two widely used methods of sowing. The first was to toss the seed by hand. The second was to attach bags of seeds to animals, with holes in the bags large enough for the seeds to trickle out. Jesus' parable suggests the first method of sowing—and rocks and thorns were common problems for Bible-time farmers.

■ The mustard seed isn't the smallest seed known today, but it was the smallest seed used by Palestianian farmers and gardeners. From this tiny seed, and under the right conditions, the tree, or plant, could grow as tall as ten fee.

■ Mark 4:10-12 seems to suggest that the parables weren't meant to enlighten people, but to cause the unbeliever to become even more unbelieving. The truths in the parables might have the effect of turning off the unbeliever. If he or she won't accept or believe in Jesus, then he or she won't understand His parables. It has to do with the condition of one's heart and its willingness to receive God's truth.

WEEK 5 The "If Onlys"

Overview

• To discover the power Jesus has.

• To understand that a person can come to Jesus with the smallest amount of faith, with doubts, and with needs—and find help and salvation.

Scripture: Mark 5

1 Getting Started

Housekeeping

Make any necessary announcements, then point out that this week finishes the first unit in the Book of Mark. Recap the rest of the study for the group: the middle unit, "In High Gear," picks up the pace of Jesus' ministry, and the third unit, "Grand Finale," follows Jesus during His last week on earth.

Icebreaker

You'll need some blank paper and markers for this icebreaker activity. Hand out the paper and markers to group members, and explain that they're to design personalized license plates. Encourage group members to come up with a creative combination of letters and numbers. For example, KLU S could stand for "clueless," as in "I have no idea of what I'm going to do with my life." Or, the old stand-by 1 WAY for "Jesus is the only way to God." Or, N LUV for the romantics in the group.

 ## Opening

The song "Majesty" by Jack Hayford fits with this week's study of Jesus' power and compassion. Here are the words to it.

Majesty, worship his majesty,
Unto Jesus be all glory, power, and praise.
Majesty, kingdom authority
Flows from his throne unto his own
His anthem raise!
So exalt, lift up on high
the name of Jesus!
Magnify, come glorify Christ Jesus the King!
Majesty, worship his majesty!
Jesus who died, now glorified,
King of all Kings!

© 1981 by Rocksmith Music. ARR. UBP.

Here's a prayer you can use or adapt for this study:

Lord, You are the King of all kings and have all authority over creation. You also accept us as we are, and bring healing and salvation. Thank You for both Your majesty and gentle love to us. In Your name. Amen.

3 Bible Study

 ## Focus

 Take a few minutes to talk about the two questions in the introduction to this week's Bible study (see page 37 in the journal).

In both cases, a person might not feel "good enough" to come to Christ. The perfectionist might feel he or she has to get over this one little bad habit before coming to Christ. The non-perfectionist might feel that the bad habit is so bad that he or she could never come to Christ. Also, talk about other things that keep people from admitting their need for Jesus, such as total self-sufficiency, stubbornness, and basically, pride.

Say something like this: **As you probably noticed, Mark 5 was about three very different people, but as we'll discover all three had something in common.**

Dig In

To set the stage for Jesus' encounter with the demon-possessed man, discuss question three in the Bible study journal.

The action takes place in the region of the Gerasenes, among the tombs (see Inside Insights for a comment about this region).

Group members probably will remember that Jesus' encounter with the demon-possessed man took place the morning after He calmed the storm.

As you talk about the events of Mark 5, group members may want to refer to their answers for questions five and six in the Bible study journal (see pages 41 and 42).

Leader's Tip: When you talk about Jesus' encounter with the demon-possessed man, be aware of people's fascination with the devil and demon possession. The Bible is clear in presenting the reality of Satan and his evil hosts, and just as clear in presenting Jesus' power over Satan. As you talk about demon-possession, don't go overboard; keep the goal in mind—Jesus' power over evil.

Describe the extremes, both externally and internally, of the man who was possessed by demons. (For example, he lived in the tombs, obviously isolated from everyone. He had been chained hand and foot, but no one could bind him anymore, because he tore the chains apart. He was stronger than anyone and overpowered people. He roamed the tombs night and day.)

How do you think the man must have felt in his few clearheaded moments?

Why do you think this man was so degraded?

You might want to mention that a purpose of demon possession is to torment and destroy the divine image in humanity. This only shows Satan's intense hatred of God.

The demon-possessed man called Jesus, "Son of the Most High God." Where had Jesus heard that before, and who did He really address?

It was back in Mark 3, when Jesus was healing people and confronting evil spirits (also in Mark 1:23-26). These evil spirits recognized who Jesus was and realized that He alone had the power to overthrow them. Jesus confronted the evil spirits and demanded that they leave the man.

In your opinion, what is the high point in the drama?

Look at the different reactions to the man's healing. Why do you think the townspeople were afraid and wanted Jesus to leave the region?

You might want to point out that the pigs' demise was a big concern too. With a herd of two thousand, the pigs were big business so the swineherders may have been upset at the loss of business.

In earlier chapters, Jesus wanted people who were healed to keep quiet. Why do you think He told the ex-demoniac to tell everyone what had happened. Do you honestly think the man could have kept quiet?

One thought is that this miracle took place in a Gentile region, where there was little danger that ideas about the Messiah would be circulated.

Now, in Mark's typical style, he jumps to two other encounters Jesus had. Say something like this: **The rest of the chapter looks at two very different people: Jairus and his daughter and an unnamed woman.**

You might want to share some of the information in Inside Insights about the nature of the woman's disease; then as a group, list some of the differences between Jairus and the woman. (It's okay to speculate a little.)

For example, Jairus was rich (he was a ruler of one of the synagogues), the woman was poor (she had spent all she had on doctors); Jairus was accepted in the community, the woman was an outcast; Jairus had a family and a daughter he obviously cared about, and the woman was alone.

Jairus gets to Jesus first; then this woman interrupts Him. How would you have felt if you had been Jairus trying to hurry Jesus off to your house?

Let's deal with this woman. What motivated her to come to Jesus?

Her overwhelming and desperate need to be healed. She didn't even care if Jesus spoke to her; she just wanted to be healed. Perhaps the woman thought that there was something magical about touching Jesus.

Why do you think Jesus wanted to see who had touched Him? Get group members to look at Jesus' tender reaction to this terrified woman: He acknowledged her faith in front of everyone, and He wanted to reassure her that she had truly been healed.

Back to Jairus. What motivated him to come to Jesus?

Like the woman, he had a desperate need for his daughter to be healed.

What did Jesus emphasize for both Jairus and the woman?

How would you describe the woman's and Jairus's faith?

Both had faith, and they also had huge needs.

What does this tell you about how a person may come to Jesus?

What does this tell you about Jesus?

 Now that you've looked at the three encounters in Mark 5, get several group members to read the before-and-after stories they wrote for question seven in the journal.

Reflect and Respond

Think about the ways you saw Jesus' power in Mark 5.

How would you describe it when Jesus confronted the legion of demons?

How would you describe it when the woman touched Jesus' clothes?

And how would you describe Jesus' power when He raised Jairus's daughter from the dead?

Get group members to look at the results of Jesus' power in each situation. The demoniac was in his right mind; the woman felt in her entire body that she was freed from her suffering; and Jairus's daughter came back to life! Wow!

What does His power mean to you personally? Give people time to think before sharing their responses with the group.

3 Sharing and Prayer

As you close, give group members a chance to talk about what's going on in their lives and what they would like the group to pray about. If you've been praying about some specific requests, this might be a good time to ask for an update.

Before people depart, remind them to complete Week 6 for the next small group meeting.

Difficult People

Overview

• To explain why Jesus and John the Baptist were often treated with disrespect.

• To show that Jesus comes to people in their need and doubts.

Scripture: Mark 6

1 Getting Started

Housekeeping

Welcome each person to the meeting. Make any necessary announcements, and then get started.

Icebreaker

Make sure everybody has a piece of paper and something to write with. Ask group members to think about one of their favorite things to do, something they're really good at. Examples might include sports, drama, debate, playing a musical instrument, etc.

Once everyone has chosen an activity, have group members write extremely unfair reviews of their performances in these areas. Members might want to imitate Siskel and Ebert as they create their reviews. When people have finished their evaluations, ask volunteers to read them out loud; then explain why the criticisms are unfair.

To get the people ready for the study, ask: **People can be unfair for a lot of** reasons. **What are some of them?** People can be unfair because they stand to gain if they cheat; they might be unfair just because they don't like the person, or they're offended by that person's beliefs.

Leader's Tip: In a small group, never force anyone to contribute; always let people know that they can pass at any time. At the very least, make sure people say hello to each other. Beyond this, don't push anyone beyond his or her social comfort level.

Opening

If the group is up to it, you might want to sing, "I Have Decided to Follow Jesus." Here are three verses to that song. You can find this song in most hymnbooks; it's been around for a while.

I have decided to follow Jesus,
I have decided to follow Jesus,
I have decided to follow Jesus,
No turning back, no turning back.

The cross before me, the world behind me,
The cross before me, the world behind me,
The cross before me, the world behind me,
No turning back, no turning back.

Though none go with me, still I will follow,
Though none go with me, still I will follow,
Though none go with me, still I will follow,
No turning back, no turning back.

Here's a prayer to use or adapt for this week's study:

Heavenly Father, You never promised that people would treat us fairly because of our faith in You, or that life would be hassle-free. As we look at the examples of Jesus and John the Baptist, give us the wisdom to respond well when we are treated unjustly. Thank You for this opportunity to study your Word and to learn from it. In Jesus' name, Amen.

 Bible Study

Focus

Ask the people in your group how they feel about being criticized, and what happens to their motivation (see the introduction on page 47 in the journal).

As members talk about their feelings, get them to clarify the type of criticism they're talking about. After this, talk briefly about what happens to relationships where destructive criticism is constantly present.

Ask: **What's your favorite comeback to people who bug you about the way you do something?**

You might see a few smiles as people in the group think of things they'd really like to say. Encourage group members to be as polite as possible here.

At this point, you want to make a transition from criticism in general to being criticized for one's faith. In Mark 6, Jesus and John the Baptist were criticized for telling people the truth about God.

People like to hear about God's love, or that Jesus can help them with their problems. But many of Jesus' teachings rub people the wrong way. We don't want to hear about sin or admit that we need God.

When a Christian starts talking about these things, instead of attacking the message, some people will attack the messenger. This is what people did to Jesus and John the Baptist.

Dig In

 Ask group members to explain how they marked up Mark 6, and explain their section titles and summaries. Skip down to question five and see what questions people had about the chapter.

Don't panic—you don't have to answer the questions. Here's your way out—and you'll remain true to the inductive method at the same time.

As we talk about Mark 6, some of your questions probably will be answered. If not, jump in and ask your specific questions, and together, we'll look for the answers.

The discussion questions go through these major sections one at a time—No Respect for a Hometown Prophet; Jesus Sends out the Apostles; The Execution of John the Baptist; Jesus Feeds over Five Thousand; and Jesus Walks on the Water. If the people in your group don't have these exact sections, don't worry about it; the discussion questions will still work.

 Based on observations that group members made about the passage in question two, discuss the rejection of Jesus in His hometown.

Jesus' hometown was Nazareth. You might want to share some details about His town from Inside Insights. **Describe as many details about this incident as you can.**

For example, Jesus was leaving the town where He had just healed Jairus's daughter (probably Capernaum); Jesus took His disciples with Him; the events occurred on the sabbath; He was teaching in the synagogue (where most Jews would be on the sabbath); and so on.

What do you think Jesus' said that got these people so upset? The answers to this question will be pure speculation, since the Bible does not say what Jesus was teaching. Get group members to make educated guesses. Here are some of Jesus' teaching that usually got a negative reaction from people; Jesus spoke favorably of Gentiles (Luke 4:24-30); Jesus said that He preceded Abraham (John 8:58); Jesus claimed to be equal with God (John 10:25-31).

Why did the hometown folks reject Jesus? To these people, Jesus seemed as ordinary as they were. In their minds, He was putting Himself on a pedestal. His claims also threatened their religious security. Instead of responding to His message, they tried to discredit Him. They may have attributed His ability to do miracles to evil supernatural powers.

Why couldn't Jesus do a lot of miracles in this place? Encourage group members to look for Jesus' reaction in Mark 6:6—Jesus was amazed at their lack of faith. It wasn't that Jesus was unable to perform a miracle; He chose not to do a lot of miracles.

What effect do you think unbelief has on God's power? There often seems to be a connection between faith and God's power. In fact, the amazement of Jesus is mentioned one other time in Luke 7:9, where Jesus was amazed at a person's faith.

Ask group members to think about this next question, without answering aloud: **What is it about us that amazes Jesus?**

Why didn't Jesus want the apostles to take along basic provisions? There seems to be a sense of urgency to this particular mission. Jesus wanted His disciples to learn how to depend on God in extraordinary circumstances. They also were to depend on the hospitality of the people to whom they preached.

What's the point for Christians today? What are some things Jesus tells us not to take along in order to be credible messengers?

Get group members to talk about the extra baggage some Christians carry that don't help the cause of Christ.

 Go over questions three and four in the journal to get a basic understanding of how the main characters relate to each other.

Ask: **How does the use of a flashback in this section make things more dramatic?**

Why was Herod so paranoid about the presence of Jesus in his jurisdiction?

You might want to mention the earlier Herod who tried to have the baby Jesus killed. The current Herod might have thought that Jesus would seek revenge. Obviously, this Herod had mixed feelings about the execution of John the Baptist, and thought his decision was coming back to haunt him. You might want to share some information about the Herods in Inside Insights.

As a group, trace Herod's spiritual journey, and where he eventually ended up. Look for clues to what motivated Herod, his emotions and reactions, and who influenced him.

Think about people you know who are spiritually sensitive. Who or what might keep them from coming to Jesus?

Leader's Tip: You don't have to do this all the time, but when someone says something that is profound, acknowledge that in front of the group. You might say something like, "That's a really good point," or "I hadn't thought of that." Hopefully, the other people in the group will pick up on your example, and start doing the same thing.

 Ask the group members to give their versions of what happened at this event (question seven, page 53 of the Bible study journal). Talk about what the people might have been thinking before and after this miracle.

Why did Jesus ask the disciples to feed the people? Perhaps He wanted them to think about their inadequacy apart from God's power. Later on, Jesus said this event was intended to build the faith of the disciples (Matt. 16:8-11).

Why do you think so much food was left over? The miracle showed God's ability to fully satisfy any appropriate need; the remaining food left no doubts about the adequacy of God's provision.

Why was Jesus so popular during this time of His ministry? Jesus was demonstrating the power of God in His healing; people wanted this for themselves. The more Jesus taught hard things about God's truth, the less popular He became.

These questions address the last section, Jesus Walks on the Water.

Why do you think Jesus was so quick to get the disciples away from the crowds? He was trying to get them to rest earlier, and had again been interrupted. Actually, the phrase "Jesus made his disciples get into the boat," indicates some pressure on Jesus' part. He had to force the disciples into the boat. The crowd was probably fired up after the miracle and wanted to make Jesus their king right then and there, and the disciples would have only added fuel the fire.

Who made the disciples get into the boat? And then what happened? Point out that it was the disciples' obedience to Jesus that put them in this miserable situation.

What does this whole episode at sea tell you about obeying Jesus? About Jesus Himself?

Reflect and Respond

Talk about question nine in the Bible study journal, and have group members read how they filled in the sentence in the Scripture text. Ask someone to read Mark 6:51, 52.

Did their reaction surprise you? Why or why not? Why did the disciples react this way to Jesus?

Mark 6:52 states two reasons for the disciples' reaction: they didn't understand about the loaves and fishes and their hearts were hardened. In some ways, the disciples were like Jesus' opponents, who just couldn't figure out Jesus, so they chose not to believe. If the disciples had understood the miracle of the feeding of the crowd, then they wouldn't have been surprised at all that this same all-powerful Jesus could walk on water.

The disciples couldn't believe that Jesus would really come to them in their need. So what that He just fed over five thousand people. He can't do anything about this storm.

Have you ever had a similar reaction to Jesus? You just don't believe He'll meet your needs or answer your prayers.

Encourage group members to talk openly and honestly about their

INSIDE
INSIGHTS

■ Nazareth was a ghetto-type town in southern Galilee. It didn't have a very good reputation. The townspeople spoke in a dialect that was difficult to understand, and they tended to be irreverent and morally loose. When Nathanael, an apostle-to-be, learned that Jesus was from this town, he asked "Can anything good come from there?" (John 1:46).

■ The expression "shaking the dust off of one's feet" is still used today. To the Jewish apostles, it meant treating these Jewish towns as if they were unclean, pagan cities.

■ The Herods were the ruling family over Israel during the first half of the first century. They were viewed as traitors by the Jews, and puppets by the Roman empire. Herod the Great tried to have Jesus killed when He was a baby. He died about two years after Jesus was born. One successor was his son Herod Antipas, the Herod of Mark 6. Herod the Great had another son, half-brother of Antipas, Philip the Tetrarch. Philip was the former husband of Antipas' wife, Herodias.

■ Some superstitious Jews believed in ghosts. Though the occult practice of spiritism was forbidden in the Old Testament, the belief in ghosts was still very popular. The appearance of such spirits during the night was considered especially threatening.

reactions to Jesus. Sometimes it really does seem as if Jesus answers everyone else's prayers, but yours. This would be a good time for people to mention some of the things they don't understand about Jesus (the last part of question nine in the journal).

To wrap up the small group study, say something like this: **It's okay to have questions about who Jesus is, but if you don't understand Him because you're choosing not to understand, then you might have some problems.**

Point out that Jesus comes to people in their terrifying storms, in their doubts, and in their needs. He wants to meet their needs.

3 Sharing and Prayer

In the closing minutes, give the group members a chance to talk about what's going on in their lives, and to give their prayer requests. Ask people to report any answers to prayer.

Before people start to leave, remind them to work on Week 7 for the next small group time.

Cover Up

Overview

• To explain why Jesus does not tolerate religious phoniness.

• To show why wearing "masks" can hurt spiritual growth.

Scripture: Mark 7

1 Getting Started

Housekeeping

Welcome each person to the meeting. Make any necessary announcements, and then get started.

Icebreaker

For this activity, each person in your group will need two pieces of construction paper, cut into 8" half-circles. (You'll need to work on this before the group meets.) Make sure everyone has a marker or pen. On one of the half-circles, ask group members to draw a "phony" smile. On the other circle, have them draw pouty mouths.

When people have finished, pair them off. Ask partners to have a short conversation about any topic of their choice. (You might want to give some suggestions such as a current story in the news, or an activity that partners have in common. Any topic is fair game as long as it's not about specific people.) During the conversation, each partner must hold up one of his or her masks. If a person holds up the happy face, he or she must be overly optimistic about the topic (that is, "everything is great, everything is going to work out fine," and so on). If a person holds up the pout, he or she must be overly pessimistic. ("Everything stinks, nothing is going to work out, everybody's going to lose.")

Allow two or three minutes for these conversations, then bring the group together. Ask people how they felt hiding behind a mask.

Opening

You might want to open the Bible Study by reading this verse from the hymn, "Just As I Am."

Just as I am, tho' tossed about
With many a conflict, many a doubt
Fightings and fears, within, without,
O Lamb of God, I come! I come!

Here's a prayer to use or adapt for this week's study:

God, sometimes we want to put on masks when it hurts too much to be real. Give us the courage to be honest about how we feel. Give us the wisdom to know when it's appropriate to express those feelings. Thank You that You accept us just as we are, and help us to become more like Your Son, Jesus, in whose name we pray. Amen.

2 Bible Study

Focus

Go around the group and talk about the different kinds of "masks" that people wear. Be careful here—some people may be wearing their "masks" right now, and may not want to take them off.

Ask: **Are all masks bad? If not, when do they become bad?** Not all masks are bad. Sometimes we just don't know people well enough to be completely vulnerable with them. Sometimes, however, people will deliberately wear masks in order to deceive people. These are the masks of hypocrisy.

Jesus had a unique way of removing the masks of hypocrites.

Dig In

Ask group members how they divided up the chapter, giving their titles and section summaries. Based on observations that people made about the chapter (question two of the Bible study journal), talk about the following questions about the hypocrisy of the Pharisees.

What's going on between Jesus and the Pharisees in this section? The Pharisees had come to Jesus, probably not to hear Him teach, but rather to confront Him on something. There's a parenthetical statement that explains a Jewish tradition. Jesus quoted from the Old Testament, and called the Pharisees hypocrites. Jesus exposed their practice of "lawfully" blowing off their responsibility to their parents. After confronting the Pharisees, Jesus called the crowd to Him to further explain His teaching about what makes a person "unclean."

What was the main complaint Jesus had about the Pharisees?

Why did this turn the Pharisees into hypocrites?

A good example of what Jesus was talking about was how the Pharisees got around the law of supporting their elderly parents.

You may want to share the information about "Corban" from Inside Insights. Part of fulfilling the fifth commandment of honoring one's father and mother was taking care of them in their old age. Apparently, one of the traditions of the Pharisees was "dedicating" part of their income to God. Once money had been dedicated to God, no one other than the person dedicating the money could benefit from it. This was a "religious" way of excusing oneself from taking care of family. How convenient.

Take a couple of minutes to talk about the different ways people misuse Christianity as a cover-up for their own selfish ends. While on earth, Jesus exposed this religious sham.

Why do you think Jesus called the crowd over to Him to explain what just happened? The Pharisees probably weren't interested in learning why Jesus thought they were hypocrites. Jesus wanted the people observing this exchange to know what made a person "clean" and "unclean."

What's the significance of Jesus' explanation?

The Jews had ceremonial regulations about what they could and could not eat. By the time Jesus had arrived on the scene, these symbols had served their purpose. "Unclean" foods, like pork, symbolized the distinctness of Israel from other peoples. Since Mark was writing to Gentiles, he did not want them to feel obligated to participate in Jewish ritual and tradition in order to be accepted by God. See Inside Insights for background on kosher foods.

Have someone in the group turn to Mark 7: 20-23 in his or her Bible and read it aloud. Get the group to explain the differences between the ceremonial washing and the kind of cleanliness Jesus was describing.

Discuss this question: **If there were no one around (like Satan) to tempt people to sin, would there still be evil in the world?**

People like to blame whatever is bad about society on the devil. That's because they make the assumption that people are basically good. The truth is, evil comes from the human heart.

Jesus cut to the chase. External cleanliness was worthless until you solved the root problem—internal sinfulness. How would you deal with the root cause of sin?

As group members give their opinions, take advantage of the discussion to talk about the Gospel—the only way approved by God to deal with sin. The Reflect and Respond section in Week 2 has a good explanation of salvation.

The next set of questions focus on the faith of the Gentile woman.

Why do you think Jesus wanted to keep His presence a secret? As we read in chapter 6, Jesus and the disciples were extremely busy in their ministry; people placed a lot of demands on them. Perhaps Jesus just wanted to get some rest.

What did you think Jesus was talking about when He said it wasn't right to take the children's bread and toss it to dogs? First of all, remember that the woman was a Gentile. She wasn't Jewish. According to Jewish slang at the time, the children would have referred to Israel, and the dogs to Gentiles. The Gospel was to be given to the Jewish people first, then the Gentiles.

Why did Jesus like the reply of the woman? The woman picked up on Jesus' metaphor, and turned it around to her advantage. Her reply also showed the depth of her faith in Jesus' ability to heal. She believed that Jesus could heal her daughter, and she wasn't going to settle for anything less.

As a group, describe some of the important details of Jesus' healing the man who was deaf. **Why do you think Jesus touched the man?**

Mention that people who were physically disabled in the first century often were not touched, especially lepers. They were considered outcasts. Jesus physically touched many people that He healed as a way of communicating His care, compassion, and unconditional acceptance of them.

 Ask group members to look at the chart in question five (page 59 in the journal), and talk about the different feelings the people in Mark 7 had about Jesus.

What does this tell you about the kind of people Jesus came for? Jesus doesn't come for the self-righteous, religious people, who don't believe they need Him. Jesus came for people who know they have needs and can't do anything about them—apart from Him.

Reflect and Respond

Move into this section by asking someone to look up Mark 7:6, 7 in his or her Bible and read it aloud: "These people honor me with their lips, but their hearts are far from me. They worship me in vain; their teachings are but rules taught by men."

If God is more concerned about our hearts than about rules and regulations, should we just ignore biblical guidelines like the Ten Commandments? Why or why not? Jesus said that He did not come to abolish the law, but to fulfill it. (See Matthew 5:17.) God still wants us to follow biblical guidelines, but not in order to impress others. He wants us to obey Him because we love Him, not because we want to appear more spiritual than others, or to get on God's good side.

Before closing in group prayer, lead the group in a short guided prayer, based on question ten and the Personal Prayer section of the journal. To lead a guided prayer, read the following phrases, pausing after each one to let people pray silently.

God, it's easy to pick on the Pharisees for their hypocrisy, but we're all guilty of wearing masks. Here are some of the masks we wear . . . (Pause.)

These masks are a cover-up for these sins that we confess to You . . . (Pause.)

Thank You for forgiving us through Your Son, Jesus Christ. Amen.

If you're a close group and feel comfortable being vulnerable, talk about some of the masks you wear, and then use the guided prayer.

3 Sharing and Prayer

Give group members a chance to talk about how things are going for them. Follow up on concerns that they may have mentioned in past weeks. Once old news and new news has been talked about, lead the group in a time of prayer.

As people begin to leave, be sure to remind them to work on Mark 8 in their journals for next week.

INSIDE INSIGHTS

■ This ritual of washing one's hands meant more than good hygiene to the Pharisees. This ritual supposedly affected their inward purity. They became "ceremonially unclean" during normal living. The cleansing meant they got rid of any impurities they might have picked up in the marketplace.

■ The term "Corban" was used for an offering or service that was given to God—in this case, money that was dedicated to God. By using this word in a religious vow, a Jewish son could get out of caring for his aging parents by arguing that the money was now sacred and could never again be used for anything else.

■ Leviticus 11 gives several kosher laws for Jews. Based on these laws, people couldn't eat any pork products. Other more obscure meats in these laws included dogs, bats, and owls. Most of these meats were excluded for ceremonial reasons, and some were excluded for health reasons

■ The term "Greek" was often used to describe a Gentile from any country, not just those from Greece. Obviously the woman from Syrian Phoenicia was not from Greece. She was from a part of Phoenicia that was under the control of Syria at the time, located along the eastern coast of the Mediterranean Sea.

Miracles on Demand

Overview

• To talk about Jesus' expectations for Christians.

• To show why it's dangerous to base our faith simply on miracles.

Scripture: Mark 8

1 Getting Started

Housekeeping

This is a good time to ask group members for some feedback about the small group. What do they like about the group? Anything that could be changed to make the group even better? Is the meeting time about right, or should it be longer or shorter? How are people doing in their journals?

Leader's Tip: As a group leader, you've probably invested more time in the group than others. That's great, but (you knew that was coming) try not to get defensive if other members voice legitimate complaints about the group time. Work through changes as a group.

Icebreaker

Do a brief word-association with the group. Use this list of words, or come up with your own list. Go around the group and ask each person to say the first thing that comes to mind when he or she hears these words:

- fast food

- TV

- family

- holiday

- school

- money

- date

Whether you use this list or your own, end the word-association with the word "miracle." Possible responses include, "supernatural," "magic," "on thirty-fourth street" "Cubs winning the pennant."

Opening

If the group would like to open with a song, and enough people know it, sing the first verse of "It Is Well with My Soul." Explain to the group members that this hymn was written by a Christian man who had just lost his wife and children in a shipwreck. If group members don't know this hymn, simply read the words or take the time to teach it to them. It's a classic hymn that's worth knowing.

When peace like a river attendeth my way
When sorrows like sea billows roll;
Whatever my lot,
Thou hast taught me to say
It is well, it is well with my soul.

Words by Horatio G. Spafford; Music by Philip P. Bliss

Here's a prayer to use or adapt for this week's study:

God, sometimes the miracles we think we need don't happen. During times like those, help us focus on who You are, not on what You can do for us. These things we pray in Jesus' name. Amen.

2 Bible Study

Focus

Begin today's discussion about miracles and faith by asking: **Suppose Jeannie from "I Dream of Jeannie" popped out of her bottle and announced that she would grant you three wishes. What would your wishes be?** Remind group members that there are no limits to their wishes.

When you've finished with all this wishful thinking, ask: **How do some people treat God like a cosmic genie?**

What's the danger in treating God like a genie?

Say something like this: **Whenever Jesus was asked to produce miracles on demand to prove His authority, He refused to perform. God does not want our belief in Him to be based on the miraculous things He can do for us. He wants our loyalty and faithfulness even when miracles don't happen.**

Dig In

Based on observations that the people in the group have made about Mark 8 (see questions one and two in the Bible study journal, page 66), discuss these questions about Jesus' feeding of the four thousand.

Why do you think Jesus repeated the miracle of feeding the thousands? The text says that Jesus had compassion for this crowd and was concerned about their need for food. Later on, Jesus asked the disciples to compare this feeding with the feeding of the five thousand. Apparently the disciples didn't get it the first time, and it seems that they didn't understand what happened the second time. The repetition would have helped the disciples to learn.

Why do you think the Pharisees wanted another miracle, even after Jesus had just supernaturally fed thousands of people? The text says that they made this demand in order to test Him, not out of genuine need. Perhaps the Pharisees demanded a miracle of their own so that they could feel some sense of control over Jesus. If Jesus had produced the sign they demanded, their resulting "faith" would have had a very shaky foundation.

Any ideas of what Jesus meant about the yeast of the Pharisees and Herod?
Take the time to explain some of the ideas in Inside Insights about baking
bread in the first century. Jesus was drawing an analogy from the loaf of bread
the disciples had in the boat. When yeast is introduced in a bread recipe, its
"influence" spreads throughout the entire loaf, but it cannot be seen once the
bread is cooked. It was the same way with the influence of these corrupt leaders—their influence tainted every aspect of Jewish life, but it was hard to detect.

 Go over the chart in question five in the Bible study journal, and have group
members explain the ratings they gave each character. Next, ask group
members to look for clues to how Jesus felt about the way people responded
to Him.

For example, when Jesus sighed deeply, He probably was exasperated at people's demands for yet another sign. Jesus seemed discouraged that His disciples
didn't understand the significance of what they had seen with their own eyes
(as well as eaten).

**Do you think Jesus was being too hard on the disciples? Why didn't He just
explain what He meant?**

**A lot of people today have that same kind of attitude. If Jesus would only
explain what He means, then they would believe Him. What do you think?
Is this necessarily true? Why or why not?**

It all depends on how you look at it. In some cases, once a person understands
what Jesus meant, he or she might come to Christ. Often this kind of attitude is
an excuse for not believing in Jesus.

Go around the group and ask members to supply details about the healing of
the blind man. For example, other people begged Jesus to heal the blind man,
Jesus took the blind man by the hand, Jesus spit on the man's eyes and touched
him again. The man wasn't totally healed the first time.

Why do you think Jesus had to touch this man twice? People who have been
blind for a long time, and then suddenly are able to see, might not have the
ability to interpret what they see. The second healing may have given the man
the ability to interpret what he saw.

Do you think the blind man's friends expected a healing like this? Most
likely, not. They probably expected Jesus to heal the man instantly.

What does this tell you about Jesus and the way He works?

Why did Jesus grant this request for a miracle, but not the Pharisees' request? The Pharisees' demand was a test; they did not really believe that Jesus was the Son of God. The blind man had a genuine need, and the people who brought him to Jesus were not trying to test the Lord.

Why do you think Jesus didn't heal everyone in Jerusalem who was sick? Think about the other times Jesus healed people too. Jesus healed some people because He had compassion on them, and to demonstrate His God-given authority. Jesus was more concerned about permanently healing the spiritual diseases caused by sin, than with temporary physical healing. That's why He told the paralytic that his sins were forgiven and honored the woman's faith.

What was the significance of Peter's confession? Peter had understood for himself who Jesus really was. Peter recognized Jesus as God's Messiah, not just another prophet.

Why didn't Jesus come right out and say who He was? You might want to mention that the best way to learn is to discover the truth for yourself (sound familiar?). Jesus wanted to see if His disciples would be able to sift through the false ideas about Him, and acknowledge Him as the promised Messiah.

How do people today describe Jesus? For example, Jesus was a good moral teacher, a religious fanatic, a prophet. Christians believe that Jesus is the Messiah, the Son of God.

 Based on what group members wrote down for question five in the journal, talk about some of the conflicts in the passage and who's causing them. The obvious conflict is between Jesus and the Pharisees.

Were you surprised at any of the conflicts? It does seem strange that Jesus and Peter would have conflict, especially after Peter's great declaration: "You are the Christ."

What do you think Peter was reacting to?

Peter had just confessed that Jesus was the Christ, the Messiah. All this talk about Jesus' suffering, rejection, and death on the cross went against Peter's expectations of the coming Messiah. As far as Peter was concerned it would be totally wrong for Jesus to suffer.

Like many other first-century Jews, Peter wanted a messiah who would over-throw the oppressive Roman Empire.

What do you think Jesus was reacting to?

Way back at the beginning of Mark's Gospel, there's a reference to Jesus' temp-tation in the desert (see Mark 1:12, 13). If you'd like, have someone turn to Matthew 4:8-10 and read these verses aloud. Satan was tempting Jesus to take a short-cut around the suffering, and still get all the kingdoms of the world. There wasn't a need for Jesus to suffer and die on the cross. In a way, Peter was doing the same thing. His plans for Jesus didn't involved suffering and death.

Why did Jesus predict His death in such detail for the disciples? Jesus want-ed to prepare His followers for His inevitably violent death. When it was all over, they would be able to look back and say, "Oh yeah, He told us this would happen."

Say something like this: **Basically, there are two questions we have to answer: Who do we say Jesus is, and are we ready to deny ourselves, take up our crosses, and follow Him?**

 ## Reflect and Respond

Move into this section by reading Mark 8:34, 35 from your Bible.

 As a group, talk about your different answers to question nine in the journal.

Ask: **Which would be hardest for you and why?**

When everyone has had a chance to talk who wants to, say something like this: **Because Jesus is the Christ, God's Son, He has the right to ask His fol-lowers for a radical commitment like this. But we're probably all over the place in our levels of commitment to Jesus.**

Explain that you're going to have a time of individual prayer before the group prayer. Say: **I'm going to read some generic responses to Jesus' radical call. When you hear one that describes pretty much how you feel, start talking to the Lord about it. And remember, Jesus accepts just as we are.**

Here are the responses; read them one at a time, pausing after each one.

- This is all new to me. I feel . . .

- I still have lots of questions. One of them is . . .

- I want to, but . . .

- I'm ready to make the commitment, and . . .

After a couple of minutes of silence, say, "Amen," and move into the group sharing and prayer.

3 Sharing and Prayer

As you close today's study, let people share any final thoughts they might have. If someone would like to share some news, now might be a good time to do it. Ask for any prayer requests, and then lead a time of prayer with your group.

Remind your group to work on Mark 9 in their journals for next week.

Glory Days

Overview

- To show that Jesus' radical claims have radical effects on His followers.
- To discover what it means to be "great" in God's eyes.

Scripture: Mark 9

1 Getting Started

Housekeeping

Take a minute to go over the small group schedule for the last third of this study. Do the meeting times still work for everyone? If you're rotating meeting in people's houses or apartments, does the schedule still work? Juggle things around if you need to, make any other announcements, then get started.

Icebreaker

Ask each person in the group to come up with three qualities the most spiritual Christian would possess. Combine all the qualities for the judging standards. Criteria might include: humble, tells others about Jesus, serves other people, has a forgiving attitude, is a peacemaker.

Talk about this hypothetical situation. **Suppose we actually gave out "The Most Spiritual Christian Award." How do you think this person would feel? How would other Christians feel toward this person? Would accepting the award be grounds for disqualification?**

Opening

If the group feels like singing, lead them in the short song, "Jesus, Name Above All Names." You probably can find this song in most hymnbooks.

Jesus, name above all names,
Beautiful Savior, glorious Lord,
Emmanuel, God is with us,
Blessed Redeemer, Living Word.

Words and music by Naida Hearn. © 1974, 1978 Scripture in Song, admin. by MARANATHA! MUSIC. All rights reserved.

Sing the song a second time as your opening prayer, or here's a prayer to use or adapt for this week's study:

Jesus, Your Name is above all names. But You didn't let that stop You from serving others. Teach us how to serve others, and help us to discover what it means to be great in the eyes of God. Amen.

◼2◼ Bible Study

Focus

Go around the group and ask people how they described their "fifteen minutes of fame." Perhaps some people in the group may already have experienced some fame and notoriety. Ask these people what they had to do for their "moment of glory." How did they feel once the fame had passed?

Ask: **What are some things people are willing to do in order to achieve fame?** Some people become famous because of their hard work and willingness to help others. Others are willing to make any compromise as long as they get a chance to be in the spotlight. Ask group members to name people who reflect both ways of becoming famous. You also might want to talk about people who have become household names lately because of what they did.

After everyone's had a chance to contribute, say something like this: **Most people want recognition for their accomplishments, and there's nothing wrong with that. Some people, however, want to be noticed for the wrong reasons. They want to be put on a pedestal in order to communicate the message: "I am more important than you."**

Jesus knew what it meant to be the greatest. God, His Father, had publicly affirmed Him in a blaze of glory. Jesus could do miracles. But He never hogged center stage.

Dig In

Ask group members to explain how they divided up Mark 9. Call on a couple people to give their titles for each of the sections. If anyone titled a section "The Transfiguration," you might want to talk about what the word means. According to Webster's dictionary, the word "transfigure" means "to give a new and typically exalted or spiritual appearance to; transform outwardly and usually for the better."

Ask: **Does this definition fit what happened to Jesus on the mountain?**

Actually, it is a good description of what happened to Jesus. Have group members give their detailed descriptions (question two in the Bible study journal, page 75). Here are some extra comments, based on the text notes of Matthew 17:1-9 (Matthew's parallel account to Mark 9:2-13) in the New International Version Study Bible.

• The Transfiguration was a revelation of the glory of the Son of God, a glory now hidden, but to be fully revealed when Jesus returns.

• It was a confirmation of the hard things Jesus had just been teaching about His suffering and death and taking up the cross.

• It benefitted the disciples who were down after Jesus reminded them of His impending suffering and death. This only happened a week after Jesus predicted His death, and Peter's little scolding of Jesus.

Come up with a group consensus of the two most spectacular details of the Transfiguration. Group members may lobby for anything they want, but in the end, there should be general agreement.

Talk about the significance of the event, and its effect on Peter, James, and John (see questions three and four in the journal). Ask: **Suppose you were on the mountain. How do you think this would have affected you?**

Have group members look at the start of Mark 9. Ask: **What do you think Jesus meant when He said that some of those standing there would not die until they saw the power of God? Did this make sense to you when you first read it?**

Jesus' statement makes better sense in light of the Transfiguration, and He was probably referring to it, since it happened a week later. Some Christians believe that Jesus may have been talking about Pentecost, when the Holy Spirit came down upon the disciples.

Of all the people in the Old Testament, why did Moses and Elijah appear with Jesus? There's more common knowledge about Moses than Elijah. Moses was given the Ten Commandments and he delivered God's people out of slavery in Egypt. On the mountain, Moses was the representative of the Old Testament covenant and the promise of salvation. Elijah was the representative of the prophets and appears as the restorer of all things.

What do you think the three of them talked about? Mark 9 doesn't give a clue to the conversation, so ask someone to look up Luke 9:31 in his or her Bible and read it. The word "departure" is a euphemism for Jesus' approaching death.

Why did Peter want to build three shelters? Peter really didn't have any idea what to say, so he could have said the first thing that popped into his head. He did have a reputation for saying the wrong thing at the wrong time.

Perhaps, at the time, Jerusalem was celebrating the Feast of Tabernacles, where everyone lived in booths for a week. Perhaps Peter thought that Moses and Elijah would like a place to stay! You might want to talk about the details of this festival described in Inside Insights.

Why do you think Jesus wanted to keep this event a secret? Jesus wanted people to accept Him for who He was, not because they feared His power, or because He could do something miraculous for them.

As Peter, James, and John were coming down the mountain, they were discussing what Jesus meant about "rising from the dead." What do you think the disciples talked about?

This wasn't the first time Jesus mention His resurrection, but what bothered the disciples more was the fact that Jesus had to suffer and die before He would rise from the dead.

What was Jesus frustrated about?

Apparently the disciples couldn't cast out the demon from the boy, because they did not have faith in God's power. Even though they had witnessed Jesus' miracles, they still had little confidence in His supernatural abilities.

What can you say about the faith of the man who asked for help with his unbelief? The man believed Jesus, but recognized his unbelief. Jesus never condemns honest doubts, as long as those doubts motivate us to discover the truth.

What seems to be on Jesus' mind as He and His disciples went on the way? In contrast, what's on the disciples' minds?

Jesus was thinking about His suffering and death; His disciples were arguing about who was the greatest.

What does this tell you about Jesus? About the disciples?

Even though the disciples kept quiet about their argument, Jesus knew what they were talking about. As far as Jesus is concerned, what makes someone great? How do you feel about this?

Position and power have no place in Jesus' upside-down values system. From His perspective, the way to greatness is through serving others.

Leader's Tip: When you ask an opinion question, expect to get opinions—informed opinions, that is. Avoid declaring someone's opinion as right or good. If you have questions about what a person says, ask him or her to clarify it a bit more.

 Choose a group member to read his or her list of Jesus' radical statements (question seven of the Bible study journal), and explain it. Encourage some give-and-take here, with other people jumping in to explain the statements they chose, and why.

This would be a good time to ask if group members have any questions about Mark 9. For example, does Jesus really want people to cut off a foot or hand that causes them to sin? (No. Jesus is using this shocking illustration in order to show the seriousness of sin. Plucking out one eye will not prevent a person from sinning with the other eye. Jesus wants us to perform "spiritual surgery" on the wrong motivations and desires that cause us to sin.)

After you've investigated the text for answers, ask group members what they discovered about Jesus; then discuss this question: **What one truth in this chapter would you want someone to really understand about Jesus and following Him?**

Leader's Tip: Most small-group leaders don't want to come off as a "know-it-all." Sometimes this is hard to avoid, since the leaders usually do more studying, and have more information. One way to avoid this perception is to name your sources. For instance, you might say, "According to these Inside Insights notes . . ." That way, the source is the "know-it-all," not the leader.

 ## Reflect and Respond

 Go around the group and talk about the different characters people identified with and why (see question nine in the journal). Also get people to talk about what they discovered about themselves and their relationships with Jesus.

When people have finished sharing, say something like this: **Mark 9:35 might be the most self-revealing verse in this chapter, because everyone wants to be first and to be considered great.** Ask someone to read Mark 9:35 in his or her Bible: "If anyone wants to be first, he must be the very last, and the servant of all."

What have you discovered about what it takes to be great in the eyes of God? And how could you practice it? Even though God honored Jesus in a blaze of glory, Jesus did not stop doing ordinary things, or even unpleasant things like casting out demons. If we want to be "first" in God's eyes, we have to be willing to do humble things (like welcoming little children who may or may not give back to us). Being a servant doesn't mean that you let people walk   all over you. It does mean always taking the interests of others into consideration—sometimes that means temporarily setting your interests aside so that others can have what they need.

3 Sharing and Prayer

Allow a few minutes at the end of your study to allow people to talk about how things are going for them. Take prayer requests. When all the requests have been made, lead in a time of prayer with your group.

Remind your group to work on Mark 10 in their journals for next week.

INSIDE INSIGHTS

■ Peter may have wanted to set up booths if Jerusalem was celebrating the Feast of Tabernacles. This feast was one of the major festivals of the year for Jews (see Leviticus 23:42). People lived in booths for seven days, symbolizing God's protection over and provision for Israel. These small tabernacles, or shelters, were made of tree branches, and reminded the Israelites of the booths their ancestors lived in shortly after the Exodus.

■ God spoke to the witnesses of the Transfiguration through a cloud. In the Bible, a cloud is often used to symbolize God's presence, and His power and rule over the world. God appeared to the people of Israel in a cloud (Exod. 19:9; 24:15; 40:34). Jesus said that He would return visibly in a cloud, just as He left (Luke 21:27; Acts 1:9).

■ During the first century, exorcists of Jesus' day appeared to cast out demons by casting spells, appealing to demons with more authority, or using pungent mixtures. Jesus simply commanded demons to leave.

■ The "Son of Man" was Jesus' favorite title for Himself; He uses it 81 times in the Gospels. The title not only points to His humanity, but also identifies Him as the Son of Man in Daniel 7:13. When Jesus used this name to describe Himself, it usually had something to do with the end times.

Loopholes

Overview

- To talk about the different levels of commitments people make to God.
- To realize that following Jesus demands a total commitment to Him.

Scripture: Mark 10

1 Getting Started

Housekeeping

How are you and your coleaders feeling about the small group time? Do any of you want to take a break? Or, better yet, are there other people who would like to become involved in group leadership? If you'd like, talk informally to a few group members to see if they would like to help lead the small group, or take on extra responsibilities.

Make any necessary announcements, then get started.

Icebreaker

A ring is a popular symbol of commitment in our culture. Before the actual Bible study begins, obtain a nice ring—a wedding ring would be best. Without any comment, pass the ring around the group, and ask each person to comment on what the ring symbolizes. Chances are you'll get a variety of comments on the nature of commitment.

When the wedding ring has gone around the circle, pull out a ring made out of a paper clip (you'll have to make this ahead of time, and make it look as crummy as possible). Pass the paper clip ring around, and ask each person to answer this question: **What type of commitment would this represent?**

Say something like this: **During a lifetime, we will make hundreds of commitments. Some will be fairly insignificant; others will be major, life-changing commitments. Some commitments will be made with greater care than others. And, in case you haven't figured it out already, commitment is a significant part in following Jesus.**

Leader's Tip: If you want to expand this activity, ask group members to talk about objects that represent commitment to them. These might include journals, a paycheck, a photo, a calendar, etc.

 ## Opening

If you would like to sing a song, sing the last verse of "Come Thou Fount of Every Blessing." Or, you may just read the words.

O to grace how great a debtor
Daily I'm constrained to be!
Let thy goodness, like a fetter,
Bind my wandering heart to thee:
Prone to wander, Lord, I feel it,
Prone to leave the God I love;
Here's my heart, O take and seal it;
Seal it for Thy courts above.

Words by Robert Robinson.

Share this fact about the author of this hymn: Years after writing these words, he abandoned his faith. Say: **Commitment is more than just poetic language; it is a promise to remain loyal no matter what.**

Here's a prayer to use or adapt for this week's study:

Heavenly Father, we make a lot of promises. Some we keep, and some we break. Thank You, dear God, for Your faithfulness to Your promises. Thank You that we can count on You with our very lives. In Jesus' name. Amen.

 Bible Study

Focus

Go around the group and ask people to read their lists of excuses for getting out of commitments. You could take a vote on the three most creative excuses. Applaud the winners, then make up some excuse for why they won't get any prizes.

Ask: **Have you ever made any commitments you were later sorry that you made? Did you try to get out of them? If so, how?** These are pretty personal questions. Depending on the people in your group, you might just want to make this a "thought" question (where no one shares an answer aloud). Even if you get one brave volunteer who answers, that probably will be enough.

To lead into the Bible study, say something like this: **Jesus could have easily gotten out of His responsibility as Savior by simply asking God to bail Him out of dangerous situations; but good thing for us, He didn't. As we'll discover in Mark 10, commitment is serious business.**

Dig In

Before getting into the specifics of this chapter, talk about question four in the Bible study journal (page 83).

 4. List all the conversations taking place in this passage. Who's talking with whom? Describe the tone of each conversation.

Here are five conversations that took place: one between Jesus and the Pharisees, one between Jesus and the rich young man, one between Jesus and the disciples, one between Jesus and James and John, and one with Jesus and Bartimaeus. (You could also divide Mark 10 into sections along the lines of these conversations.) Get several people to describe the tone of each conversation; then ask: **Which conversation would you have joined and why?**

 Now look at the motives of the Bible characters as well as Jesus' motives for responding to them the way He did (question six in the Bible study journal).

The obvious motivation of the Pharisees was to test Jesus and trip Him up. They were hostile in approaching Jesus, and Jesus didn't bother playing games with the Pharisees. The rich young man was motivated by his need to know how he could get eternal life.

Based on their conversations and motives, what can you discover about these characters' commitment level to Jesus? Group members may have to speculate a bit, but make sure their speculations are backed by Scripture.

You might want to explain to the group who the Pharisees were (see the information in Inside Insights). Ask the group members to give their observations about this section, and then ask the following questions.

If God's design for marriage didn't include divorce, why does God allow it? Actually, divorce was an accommodation to human weakness. You might want to explain to group members about how the practice of divorce was abused in Jesus' day (see Inside Insights).

Why do you think Jesus calls remarriage after divorce adultery? There are lots of opinions in the church about if, and when, it is right to remarry after divorce. In this passage, Jesus just told the Pharisees that when a man and woman marry, they become one flesh. Even though they may divorce, they still remain "one flesh" in the eyes of God.

What do you think it means to receive the kingdom of God like a little child? For example, young children tend to be trusting and open to others. Open hearts can receive Jesus as Lord and Savior. Just as children are helpless, we have realized that we can't obtain the kingdom of God through our own efforts. We have to recognize our helplessness and dependency on Jesus.

Why do you think it's hard for adults, and even people our age, to receive Jesus like a little child?

First, have group members give the rich young man's side of the story (question five, page 84 of the Bible study journal).

This young man had everything going for him. He even kept the commandments. Perhaps he was thinking, *Shouldn't all this be good enough to gain eternal life? I'm a good person. So why does Jesus want me to give up my earthly security. Besides, if it wasn't for all my money, I wouldn't be able to do half the good things I am doing now. And why should I give up the security of wealth for who knows what?*

Ask: **How did Jesus feel about this young man, and what does this tell you about Jesus?**

Do all rich people go to hell? The rich young man's problem was where he placed his ultimate security. He didn't want to give up the false sense of well-being that his money provided for him. There were many godly people in the Bible who were wealthy—Abraham, Jacob, and Job to name a few. God does not want us to put our ultimate security in anything or anyone but Him.

As a group, brainstorm some other expressions that mean the same thing as, "It is easier for a camel to go through the eye of a needle than for a rich man to enter the kingdom of God." You might want to explain this expression first, using the information in Inside Insights.

Actually, it is impossible for any human to attempt to enter the kingdom of God on his or her own. Why is it only possible through God?

This is another chance for you to explain that eternal life is a gift from God. It's all from God; it's all grace. Our part in the deal is to trust what Jesus accomplished on the cross when He died for sinful humanity.

The mistake of the rich young man was placing his ultimate security in his wealth. What do you put your ultimate security in? What gives you the greatest sense of well-being? Don't push anyone to answer this question. One volunteer's (perhaps yourself) giving an answer might be enough.

What kind of security did Jesus give Peter, after Peter declared, "We have left everything to follow you!"

How secure do you think that made Peter and the other disciples feel?

Why were the disciples still astonished at Jesus' predictions of His violent death? The disciples may still have been expecting a messiah who was going to deliver them from the oppressive Romans, not one who would hand Himself over to be killed.

What kind of baptism and drink do you think Jesus was talking about here? These are metaphors for the suffering Jesus is about to undergo. A "baptism by fire" is commonly used to described a difficult test of character. To "drink from a particular cup" is also used like this.

Why were the other disciples indignant with James and John? The other disciples may have felt that they also deserved these places of honor.

Jesus then gave His disciples a lesson in leadership. How would you sum up Jesus' teaching? For example: Do not seek positions of honor; seek first to serve, and in God's time you will be promoted.

What can you discover about God's kingdom from all this? Group members may want to explain the verses they chose as the main ones to help answer this question. (See question seven in the Bible study journal.)

Why was the crowd telling this guy to shut up? They may have felt that he was bothering Jesus. Perhaps they felt that if Jesus stopped for one beggar, He'd have to stop for all of them. Once Jesus called for the man, however, everyone changed their tune. Now that Jesus wanted to see the guy, the crowd suddenly started to encourage him.

Jesus asked the same question, "What do you want me to do for you?" on two separate occasions. In the case of James and John, he said no to the request. In the case of the blind man, Jesus did what was requested. Why do you think Jesus responded differently to the same question? James and John were asking for something that only God the Father could grant. Besides, their motives were selfish. Jesus said yes to the man's request, because he asked for it in faith. The fulfillment of his request brought glory to God; James and John wanted glory for themselves.

 ## Reflect and Respond

 Talk about what group members discovered about Jesus from His encounters with the children, the rich young man, and Bartimaeus (see question eight in the Bible study journal).

You might want to point out Jesus' motives. For example, Jesus' reply (to sell everything) came out of love for the young man. At the same time, Jesus demands total trust and total commitment from His followers.

Ask someone to read Mark 10:36, 51 in his or her Bible. **If Jesus asked you this question, what would you request? Are there any reasons that He might not give you what you asked for?**

Okay, suppose Jesus asked you to give up everything and follow Him. Would you be ready to give Him what He demanded?

If anyone wants to share his or her feelings, question nine in the Bible study journal might be a good starting point. You could also have a couple minutes of silence for group members to write down their thoughts on their readiness to follow Jesus.

3 Sharing and Prayer

Allow some time for people to talk about what's going on in their lives. Acknowledge any answers to prayer. Take any new prayer requests, and then have a short time of prayer

Before people leave, remind them to work on Mark 11 in their journals for next week.

INSIDE INSIGHTS

■ The name Pharisee means "one who is separated," and the Pharisees set themselves apart from others by the way they dressed and believed. They believed in the Old Testament law, and devoted themselves to the interpretation of it. The Pharisees thought that the rules made up by the religious leaders were to be followed as much as God's law.

■ Moses' provision for divorce was being abused by the Pharisees of Jesus' day. Some said that divorce could only occur if there was immorality; others believed that a husband could divorce his wife for any reason—like she burned the dinner. In the Hebrew culture, only the husband could "file" for divorce.

■ Some people speculate that there was a small gate in the wall that surrounded Jerusalem called the "needle's eye." A camel could fit through this gate if it went down on all fours. In the Gospel of Luke, however, Luke used the word for a surgical needle (after all, he was a doctor). Actually, Jesus' contrasted the largest animal with the smallest opening to show what humanly is impossible.

■ Drinking from someone else's "cup" was a Jewish expression that meant to share that person's fate. For Jesus, to take His cup of suffering meant that He would experience God's punishment for sins when He took the place of sinful humanity on the cross.

Fading Applause

Overview

• To begin investigating Jesus' last week on earth.

• To discover the different expectations people had about Jesus, the Messiah.

Scripture: Mark 11

1 Getting Started

Housekeeping

Welcome each person to the meeting; make any necessary announcements, then get started. Mention that there are only four weeks left in this journal, so people might want to start thinking about what they'd like to study next in the small group.

Icebreaker

Pass out index cards, and ask each person to take a card and write his or her name at the top of it, then pass it to the person on the left. Explain: **Write one encouraging thing about the person whose name appears at the top of that card. Keep passing the cards and keep writing compliments until you get your own card back.** By the way, this activity can make people feel good about themselves.

Once everyone has received and read their cards, present the following situation. **Let's suppose that we've gotten into a bad habit of gossiping. Our prayer requests have become gossip sessions. You want to confront the** problem, but don't want to risk the high opinions of others. How would you feel about being in this kind of situation?

Allow people to speak freely here. The point of the activity is to think about the cost of losing popularity for the sake of God's truth.

Leader's Tip: A good thing about being a leader is that you don't have to wait for activities like this one to encourage someone. If you tell people about the good things they've done, or about how well they do something, they will be motivated to do even more.

Opening

To begin this unit on Jesus' last week on earth, ask people if any of their stereotypes about Jesus have changed, and why.

Say something like this: **The most important question each of us has to answer is Jesus' question: "Who do you say I am?" You see, the way we answer that question may very well determine our relationship with Jesus.**

Open in prayer, using or adapting this prayer:

Dear Jesus, as we begin to investigate Your last week on earth, help us to clearly see who You are and why You came to earth. In Your name. Amen.

2 Bible Study

Focus

Go around the group and ask for opinions to the introductory question in the Bible study journal.

In some places, it is popular to have religious convictions; in others, it's viewed as narrow-mindedness.

Say: **Jesus' popularity was at an all-time high when He entered Jerusalem on Palm Sunday. In spite of that popularity, He did a lot of things that week that would eventually turn most of those people off.**

Dig In

Ask group members how they divided up Mark 11, giving sections and titles. Also talk about the shifts in tone throughout the chapter. For example, the chapter opens on a joyful note, but then switches to an angry confrontation between Jesus and the money changers.

Before talking about the specific sections, go over the character chart in question five (see page 93 in the Bible study journal). If we had filled in the chart, we would have included the crowd (people), the disciples, the money changers, and the collective character of the chief priests, teachers of the law, and the elders as the main characters.

Talk about any motives the characters may have had for the way they responded to Jesus. For example, the money changers, the chief priests, and teachers of the law were probably motivated by Jesus' clearing of the temple. But motivated to kill Jesus? That seems a little farfetched; obviously, something else was going on—and Jesus knew it.

How did Jesus know that there would be colt waiting for Him in the village?

It is possible that Jesus prearranged it. However, Jesus is God, and as God, He is all-knowing. You might want to point out that while on earth, Jesus limited His knowledge (see Matthew 24:36).

Why do you think the people were so excited about Jesus?

The crowd realized that Jesus had come in the name of God, and they had great expectations for Him, which included overthrowing the oppressive Roman rule.

Point out that the people's song was based on Psalm 118:25, 26, which celebrates Israel's victory over her enemies.

Did Jesus meet their expectations? Why or why not?

When Jesus turned Himself over to these oppressors, and did not demonstrate

His power, perhaps some of the same crowd turned against Him. He had failed to meet their expectations, but in other ways He far exceeded anyone's expectation by His offer of forgiveness of sin and eternal life.

Does Jesus' attack on the money changers seem out of character to you?

Don't let anyone get away with a yes or no answer. People have a lot of different ideas about what Jesus was really like. A person must take everything the Bible says about Jesus, and then develop an informed opinion about Him—sort of what these small group studies want to accomplish.

Why do you think Jesus' actions at the temple made the religious leaders angry enough to want to kill Him?

According to the passage, this temple incident gave the religious leaders the excuse they were looking for to kill Him. They were afraid of Jesus and the threat He posed to their authority. Jesus' accusation against the merchants indirectly accused the religious leaders who allowed it to take place. Jesus exposed their corruption to the crowds, and that threatened their standard of living and source of economic gain. He was also a threat to their false image of righteous, pious men.

These questions look at Jesus' return to the fig tree.

Does Jesus' curse on this tree seem out of character to you? After all, it's just a tree. What's the big deal?

We won't be surprised if your group had problems with this episode. Here's some extra help for you.

Some scholars criticized this event because it was unreasonable for Jesus to be looking for figs out of fig season. And it seems totally unworthy and unlikely of Jesus to react so harshly simply because He was hungry. One thing to keep in mind is that Jesus was the Creator of the universe. In this position, He has authority over all of creation—even unproductive fruit trees. According to the text notes in the New International Version, fig trees around Jerusalem normally begin to get leaves in March or April but don't produce figs until June, when all the leaves are out. This tree was an exception, because at Passover time, it was full of leaves. Perhaps the incident was a parable of judgment, with the fig tree representing Israel. A tree full of leaves normally has fruit, but this one was cursed because it didn't have any. The fact that the cleansing of the temple is sandwiched between the two parts of the account of the fig tree emphasizes the theme of judgment. Jesus' only application, however, is an illustration about believing prayer.

What do you think about Jesus' statement, "Whatever you ask for in prayer, believe that you have received it, and it will be yours"? Are there any restrictions on what we can ask God for?

As group members express their opinions, ask someone to look up James 4:3 in a Bible and read it aloud. James says that we do not receive things because we ask for the wrong reasons and motives. If we ask for things to selfishly spend on ourselves, we probably won't receive them. We are to ask for things that are clearly within God's will.

What's our part in this process of prayer?

Why wouldn't Jesus answer the question of the religious leaders? Jesus knew that these men wanted to trap him. By telling them the source of His authority (God), the religious leaders may have tried to bring charges of blasphemy against Him.

Go through the chapter as a group and map out the plan Jesus had as He began His final week on earth. Jesus purposely entered Jerusalem on a donkey, offering Himself as the Messiah, and He knew that this would provoke a reaction from the religious leaders.

Be sure to talk about the significance of this plan. (See question seven in the Bible study journal. Group members might also want to explain the way they marked up the chapter for question three.)

After you've discussed Jesus' plan, ask someone to look up and read Mark 11:9, 10, and someone else to read Mark 11:29. Ask: **How did Jesus handle His popularity?** Obviously, Jesus didn't let His popularity keep Him from teaching a very unpopular truth. He wasn't afraid to let people down when they had inaccurate expectations of Him. Jesus didn't try to get in good with the people who had power (that is, the religious leaders). In fact, it did seem as if He went out of His way to anger them. Jesus did a lot of things that threatened His popularity—and He eventually lost it.

Suppose you were in the crowd. What would you have expected from this Jesus and why?

What do you expect from Him today?

 ## Reflect and Respond

If Jesus were going to topple some "corrupt tables" in hearts of Christians today, what would those tables represent?

INSIDE INSIGHTS

■ Zechariah 9:9 is a Messianic prophecy that describes Israel's king as riding on a donkey. Jesus fulfilled this prophecy when He entered Jerusalem on a donkey. Matthew and John both quote Zechariah 9:9 (see Matthew 21:5; John 12:15). A donkey was a lowly animal of peace as well as a princely mount. Animals that had not been ridden were often used for religious purposes (Num. 19:2; Deut. 21:3, 4; I Sam. 6:7), perhaps as a symbol of purity.

■ Branches like the ones laid before Jesus were from the trees of palm, myrtle, and willow. By the way, only the Gospel of John mentions palm branches (John 12:13).

■ The money changers served as "currency exchanges" for people attending the temple to worship. Since these Jews came from all over, they needed someone to exchange their foreign currency for Jewish money acceptable for temple worship. These money changers had a monopoly on this trade, and gouged people severely. In order to sacrifice and worship, faithful people had to go through these corrupt money changers.

■ The fig tree was very common in the Mediterranean area. The tree usually has a very short trunk and thick branches. The fig is a round fruit that is very sweet, and contains several seeds. They were usually dried and stored as cakes. The fruit also had medical uses, especially for boils and other skin problems (II Kings 20:7).

You don't have to volunteer any information, but what about your own life? What tables would Jesus topple? Look over the things you wrote down for question eleven in the journal.

Be quiet for a minute, and then ask: **What are some things about Jesus that are worth shouting about?**

Get group members to call (or shout out, if they want to) some of the wonderful things about Jesus; such as He forgives sins, He accepts us, and He loves us.

3 Sharing and Prayer

Have a group time of praise, with group members thanking Jesus for some of the things they've just mentioned. When you've finished with the praise time, give the group members a chance to talk about what's going on in their lives, and to offer their prayer requests. Report any answers to prayer.

Before people start to leave, remind them to work on Mark 12 for next week.

WEEK 12 Pop Quiz

Overview

• To examine how Jesus was tested by His enemies.

• To understand that Jesus welcomes questions that are motivated from a desire to know more about Him.

• To realize that following Jesus involves loving and serving Him with heart, soul, mind, and strength.

Scripture: Mark 12

1 Getting Started

Housekeeping

Welcome each person to the meeting as he or she comes in. If you're planning to continue meeting after you've finished this particular study, this would be a good time to schedule small group times and locations. Make any other announcements, then get started.

Icebreaker

Read this situation, then ask the true-false questions that follow.

A gang member walked into a store. The woman behind the counter panicked when she saw a gun. She opened the safe and emptied the contents. The owner of the store pressed the alarm. When the police arrived, there were two people in the store.

Answer true or false to the following statements.

The woman behind the counter worked for the owner.

The gang member left with the money before the police arrived.

The gang member was the only customer in the store.

The owner and the woman let the police in.

Though the answers to these questions might seem obvious, none of them can be answered conclusively. Not enough information is given. There might have been other customers in the store. The gang member may not have had a gun. Someone else may have robbed the store. The woman and the owner may have been the same person. There might have been something other than money in the safe. The alarm might have been pressed by accident. The two people in the store might have been customers that came in after the alarm was pressed.

 ## Opening

If the group feels like singing, lead them in this verse from "A Mighty Fortress is Our God." You can find this song in most hymnbooks.

And tho' this world with devils filled
Should threaten to undo us,
We will not fear, for God has willed
His truth to triumph through us
The prince of darkness grim
We tremble not for him
His rage we can endure
For lo, his doom is sure
One little word shall fell him.

Here's a prayer to use or adapt for this week's study:

Jesus, sometimes the most difficult tests we face are from people who would like nothing better than to see us fail. As we look at the tests You faced while on earth, help us learn how to have the courage to confront our enemies, the wisdom to "pass" these tests, and the faith to trust You through it all. In Your name. Amen.

2 Bible Study

Focus

Announce to everyone that you're about to give a pop quiz on the first eleven chapters of Mark. After you've enjoyed the looks of panic on people's faces, tell them you were just kidding. Ask someone to explain how it feels to be surprised by a test and to be caught unprepared.

Say something like this: **Tests, especially the nonacademic ones, are a normal part of our lives. Some might even call them a necessary evil. What kind of test did you choose to describe your life right now?**

To get things started, you might want explain your choice first. For example, does your life feel like a multiple choice test, because you have a lot of decisions to make?

When the group has finished talking, say: **Jesus was put to the test several times during His ministry—and He always knew what to say.**

Dig In

Begin this section by looking at the chart in question two (page 101 of the Bible study journal). As a group, come up with a consensus of the people or groups who were asking their questions, their actual questions, and their motives for asking. In most cases, Jesus reveals the motives for asking.

What did you think about the way Jesus answered the questions? Why didn't Jesus act nicer and try to make everything all right between Him and the religious leaders?

You might want to mention that during Jesus' last week on earth, things intensified between Him and His enemies. Jesus purposely confronted them and exposed their hypocrisy and sin.

What is the meaning of the parable?

This parable is more complex than others, because you have to understand the social structure of first century Jewish Galilee (now we tell you). Briefly explain that in first century Galilee, large estates, owned by absentee landlords, were put in the hands of local peasants who cultivated the land as tenant farmers.

Based on group members' observations and key words and phrases, talk about the meaning of the parable. The owner, or landlord, of the vineyard was God; the vineyard was the nation of Israel. The tenants were the Jews, or better yet, their leaders; the servants were Old Testament prophets, and perhaps John the Baptist. The son is Jesus, whom the corrupt religious leaders and Pharisees wanted to kill.

Why were the religious leaders so angry?

They knew that Jesus had just spoken this parable against them. They were the "tenants" whose ancestors had killed the prophets of God, and they were the ones who wanted to kill God's Son.

What prevented these leaders from killing Jesus right then and there?

Who was in control and why?

How is Jesus like the stone that was rejected?

These questions focus on the topic of paying taxes.

What kind of trap were these men trying to catch Jesus in? They were hoping that Jesus would say that people should not pay taxes to Caesar, because Caesar did not honor the God of the Jews. Jesus saw their trap and shrewdly avoided it.

What belonged to Caesar, and what belonged to God? For those who originally heard Jesus' words, the Roman taxes belonged to Caesar, and tithes and offerings belonged to God (along with unconditional loyalty).

Warning: The following question might take up a lot of group time. Try to keep things contained.

What about us? Is it right for us to pay taxes to a government who uses the funds in ways we believe are immoral?

These questions talk about the prospect of marriage in heaven.

What kind of logic trap were the Sadducees trying to set for Jesus?

The most relevant fact about these religious leaders is that they didn't believe in the resurrection. These people assumed that in the resurrection (if there was one), life would simply continue on as it had before, only at a different level. Since it was "impossible" for a woman to have more than one husband, that must mean that there is no resurrection. Get it?

How did Jesus respond?

Jesus said that their faulty logic was a result of their ignorance of Scripture. He also explained that things would be different, because there wouldn't be marriage after the resurrection.

If a Christian husband and wife are no longer married in heaven, what will their relationship be like? We're on a roll with these kinds of questions. Even though the two people are no longer married, we might assume they will know each other better than they ever did during their earthly lives together.

Why do you think Jesus gave two commandments when the teacher of the law only asked for the one that was the most important? Jesus' reply included love for God and love for others. That's how the Ten Commandments are divided: the first four are directed toward our relationship with God, the next six toward our relationship with others. To love the Lord and to love our neighbor is foundational to God's will for our lives.

Why did Jesus treat this man's question differently than the other questions from the religious leaders?

Here are some possible answers. The man didn't have ulterior motives. He saw how Jesus handled these "tests." Jesus knew that the man accepted and believed what he just heard, and had "owned" the truth.

Why do you think the man was close to the kingdom of God, but not actually in it? The man needed more than just an intellectual understanding of God's commands—he needed to obey them.

 Take a few minutes to talk about question eight in the Bible study journal. **What would you love to ask the Pharisees or the teacher of the law who wanted to know the greatest commandment. Why?**

Some of the group's questions might help answer this next question.

Why was Jesus so down on the religious leaders? Get group members to describe contemporary teachers of the law.

Why do you think Jesus praised the widow?

See Inside Insights for more information about the situation of widows in the first century. The offerings of the wealthy cost them nothing; they hardly missed the little they gave. The widow gave a sacrifice that cost her something. King David would not offer a sacrifice that cost him nothing (II Sam. 24:24).

 Look at question nine in your journal. What did you discover about Jesus?

 ## Reflect and Respond

Move into this section by asking someone to read his or her summary statement for Mark 12 (question seven in the Bible study journal). You might want to read Mark 12:10, and then ask: **What's one truth about Christianity that you now "own," one that you truly believe, not one you believe just because your parents or pastors do?**

Allow people a few minutes to think about this one. Some group members may realize that they don't really "own" what they believe. If this is true, the question could spark some self-evaluation.

Does Jesus want us to give away every single thing we have, just as the widow did?

Leader's Tip: The best way to help people learn how to discover God's truth for themselves is to ask questions. Even if you know the answer, give other people a chance to discover the answer for themselves.

 To wrap up this study time, go around the group and share what people wrote on the two coins (see question ten in the Bible study journal). If you'd like, pass around two pennies for people to hold as they talk.

3 Sharing and Prayer

Before closing, give group members a chance to talk about how things are going. Follow up on concerns that they have brought up in the past. After everyone's had a chance to talk, lead the group in a time of prayer.

As people begin to leave, be sure to remind them to work on Mark 13 in their journals for next week.

■ Originally, the Jews only had to pay a tax for supporting the temple. Under Roman rule, the Jews paid a produce tax, a type of retail sales tax, land taxes, personal property taxes, and even a type of income tax paid directly to the Roman emperor. On top of these taxes were the charges and fees of the tax collectors, which were often excessive. Many Jews felt that it was a sin against God to pay taxes to an occupying force.

■ The Sadducees were a group of aristocratic Jewish leaders who were in charge of the temple. They were usually wealthy, and came from prominent priestly families. The name Sadducee means "righteous one." They did not believe in the resurrection, or in angels or demons. The Sadducees were often in opposition to the Pharisees and strong supporters of whoever was oppressing Israel at the time.

■ The two copper coins placed in the offering by the widow were called *lepta*, the smallest coins in circulation at the time. According to the New International Version, the coin's current value today would only be a fraction of a penny. Even though the plight of widows was terrible, most had some meager means of support. Under Jewish law, this widow was to be given shelter and food. And the little extra she had, she freely gave back to God.

I'll Be Back

Overview

• To examine the teaching about Jesus' second coming.

• To reevaluate attitudes about Jesus' return to earth.

Scripture: Mark 13

1 Getting Started

Housekeeping

Just checking, but has your group decided what they want to study next? Check out the other *Good Word* titles in the *Great Groups* series. Have a short time for announcements, then get started.

Icebreaker

Ask group members to take two or three minutes to write about an extraordinary incident that happened in their lives when they were children. If possible, they should choose an incident that others in the group probably wouldn't know about, as well as one they wouldn't mind sharing. Ask people not to talk about their stories among themselves. When they have finished, ask members to put their names at the top, and hand the stories in to you.

Pick one of the stories, and ask the author (without identifying him or her as such) and a second person to step into another room with you. Explain to the two privately that you'll read this story to the group. Each of them is to claim ownership of the story. The rest of the group will ask questions in order to figure out who is telling the truth. Tell the true author to be purposely vague; tell the "deceiver" to give involved, detailed answers. The goal is to fool the group.

Eliminate details in the story that might give away the author, like gender or geographical information. Make the story as broad as possible so it *could* apply to both people.

Opening

If the group feels like singing, lead them in the chorus of "Greater Is He That Is in Me." You can find this song in most Christian songbooks.

Greater is He that is in me,
Greater is He that is in me,
Greater is He that is in me,
Than he that is in the world.

You might want to mention that this song is based on I John 4:4: "You, dear children, are from God and have overcome them, because the one who is in you is greater than the one who is in the world."

Here's a prayer to use or adapt for this week's study:

Dear God, there are a lot of false teachers who sincerely believe what they tell others. Lord, we know that sincerity doesn't mean something is true. Give us the wisdom to avoid being deceived, and help us ask the right questions in order to know Your truth. In Jesus' name. Amen.

2 Bible Study

Focus

Begin the study by asking group members to describe some of the more strange things they've heard about Jesus' return. Remember to be nice even when you're making light of other people's claims.

Next, ask group members how they personally feel about Jesus' return (see the introductory paragraph in the Bible study journal, page 105).

Say something like this: **Jesus Himself said there would be many signs prior to His return. But some groups have gone beyond interpreting signs, and have actually calculated the exact time of Jesus' return. Ironically, one of the signs of the end is an increase in false teaching about Christ's return. Let's take a look at the things we need to watch out for.**

Dig In

Ask group members to explain how they divided this chapter up, and to give their titles and section summaries. These discussion questions apply mainly to these two sections: Signs of the End Times and Only God Knows.

Before going any further, talk about the different observations about the chapter as well as any questions people have marked (see question two in the Bible study journal, page 108).

If there is a particular passage that is tripping up everyone (like, what in the world is the "abomination that causes desolation"?), spend time talking about it. Take advantage of the extra comments and information in this meeting plan to help with the discussion.

Leader's Tip: A good leader doesn't need to supply all the answers. It's important, however, to try and find out the answers to questions in between meeting times. Check out reliable Bible commentaries or talk to other Christians who might know more about the subject than you and your group.

The following questions focus on the signs of the end times.

Why do you think Jesus took the time to explain things privately to the disciples?

Here are some ideas. Sometimes Jesus would say rather shocking things in order to get people's attention, and then see who wanted to know more.

Here when He talked about the temple being torn down, some people may have heard what He said and shrugged it off as a metaphor. Others may have heard, and decided that they didn't want to know what Jesus meant. But Peter, James, John, and Andrew wanted to know more, and Jesus was glad to explain it . . . and more.

Peter, James, John, and Andrew pulled Jesus aside in order to ask Him more about the signs of the end. If you could pull Jesus aside privately, what would you ask Him? Allow people a few minutes to talk about what they would ask Jesus. Point out that although the Bible addresses and solves many mysteries, God has purposely left some questions unanswered.

List some items described in this chapter that will happen during this age some time before Christ returns. Question five in the Bible study journal probably will help group members with this question. Here are the signs we came up with:

• Many will come claiming to be the Christ

• Wars and rumors of wars

• Earthquakes and famines

• Persecution of believers

• The opportunity to preach to one's captors

• Betrayal by family members and rebellion in families

• Hatred of believers

• The days cut short for the sake of the elect

• False Christs and prophets who can perform miracles

• The sun darkened, the moon won't give its light, the stars will appear to fall, and the heavenly bodies shaken

• All shall see the Son of Man coming in the clouds (this is no invisible return).

Next, ask someone to look up Mark 13:5, 6 in his or her Bible and read it aloud. **Say: C. S. Lewis once said, "Nothing can deceive unless it bears some plausible resemblance to reality." What do you think this means, especially in light of Jesus' warnings in this passage?**

If false teaching didn't have a ring of truth to it, no one would be taken in by it. For instance, when a Jehovah's Witness wants to convince you that Jesus returned invisibly in 1914, he or she will tell you to look at Mark 13:26. The person will point out that since Jesus was supposed to return in a cloud, no one would be able to see Him—even though the verse says that, "At that time men will see the Son of Man coming in clouds with great power and glory." False teaching that uses the Bible to back up its claims can be especially deceptive.

Ask: **Do you think it's possible for true Christians to be deceived by these false Christs and prophets? Why or why not?**

What do you think is meant by the lesson of the fig tree?

For example, Jesus uses the metaphor of a ripening tree to describe what things will be like just before He returns. We may not know the exact time of Christ's return, but we are to keep our eyes open for the signs of Christ's return. Only God the Father knows the exact day and hour.

What generation is Jesus talking about? Does every generation have a right to expect Jesus to return during its lifetime? The generation that sees the true signs of the end will not perish before the end comes. This is not meant to be a measuring device for Jesus' return, because Jesus made it clear that He didn't know exactly when He was coming back.

If Jesus is God, why doesn't He know the time of His return?

Here are some things you could add to the group discussion. As God, Jesus is omniscient, that is, He knows everything. Even though Jesus is equal with God, He willing submits to His Father's will. In this case, only God the Father knows the time of His Son's return. Jesus could have reached into His divine "database," but as a human being He also learned just as we learn (Luke 2:52).

Do you think it would help you or hinder you if you knew exactly when Jesus was coming back?

As the group kicks around ideas, ask this next question: **What does it mean to be "caught sleeping" when Jesus returns?**

Jesus does not mean literal sleep; He may very well come back in the middle of the night. In this context, sleeping means being lax in our faith and service— saying to ourselves "Oh, Jesus isn't coming for a long time; I have plenty of time to prove my faithfulness. For now I'm just going to take it easy." In that case, knowing the exact time of Jesus' return wouldn't be all that beneficial. Maybe that's why we don't know it.

What sort of response do you think Jesus wanted from His followers about all this? Encourage group members to look for the short, to-the-point commands Jesus gave. (Question five in the journal will help with this question too.)

Leader's Tip: Always encourage people to ask questions. Since God's truth is unchanging, it can stand to be challenged or questioned. And dealing with direct questions is the best way to expose false teaching. Make your group a safe place to ask questions.

Reflect and Respond

Begin this section by talking about question six in the Bible study journal.

Here are some suggested meanings for Mark 13. Be prepared for Jesus' return. Don't be fooled by false teachers who claim to be Christ. Only God the Father knows when Christ will return, so stand firm and stay alert.

Encourage people to be honest with how they feel about Jesus' return and the end times (see question seven in the Bible study journal).

As you talk about the difference this makes in your lives, ask specifically how the prospect of Christ's return should affect the way we live. For example, God does not want us to give up everything to go live up on a mountain and watch for Christ to return. This is the sort of thing some believers at Thessalonica were doing—the apostle Paul told them to get back to work (I Thess. 5:1-10). Nor are we to be obsessed with calculating the time of Jesus' return, as some groups have done. Jesus wants us to live with a constant sense of expectation for His return, but to go about our lives in such a way that honors Him.

Think about your answer to this question: What would help you anticipate Jesus' return?

You could suggest people write down their thoughts in the space by question seven. After a minute or two, move into the group sharing and prayer.

■ According to Josephus, a first-century Jewish historian, and the New International Version Study Bible notes, the massive stones of these buildings were 37 feet long, 12 feet high, and 18 feet wide.

■ A flogging before the Jewish council often meant thirteen severe strokes on the chest and twenty-six on the back with a whip or bamboo rod.

■ The "elect" are the people of God, not just a select group of believers.

■ The "abomination that causes desolation" is believed to have several historical fulfillments that precede this final desecration. Some believe this had an historical fulfillment when Antiochus Epiphanes (the last word refers to a god being "manifest") built an altar to Zeus in the middle of Jerusalem's temple. This story is in the apocryphal books of First and Second Maccabees. A similar event occurred in A.D. 40 when the Roman emperor Caligula put up a statue of himself (as god) in the temple area. The final fulfillment is understood by many to be some future manifestation of the Antichrist (as an object of worship) in Jerusalem (II Thess 2:4; Rev. 13:14, 15).

3 Sharing and Prayer

Before closing, give group members a chance to talk about what's happening in their lives. After everyone's had a chance to talk, lead the group in a time of prayer.

As people begin to leave, be sure to remind them to work on Mark 14 in their journals for next week.

Sold Out

Overview

• To investigate how Jesus handled the events leading up to His arrest and trial.

• To realize that Jesus forgives us.

Scripture: Mark 14

1 Getting Started

Housekeeping

This is the next to the last study in the Bible study journal. Make any necessary announcements first, and then say all sorts of positive things about your group. Also give group members a chance to say all sorts of positive things too.

Icebreaker

This activity is called "Friend or Foe." Choose a person to wait in another room while the other group members set up an "obstacle course." (By the way, you'll need a blindfold for this person.) As far as the obstacles go, they might just be chairs, or simply bottles on the floor. Once the course has been set up, have each person in the room count off. Even-numbered people will be "friends" and the odd-numbered people will be "foes."

Call the person back in, and explain that he or she must get instructions from the group to get around the obstacles. No one may touch the person, and only verbal instructions allowed. The "friends" will attempt to guide the person safely through the course. The "foes" will purposely give misleading instructions. The person going through the course won't know who are the friends and who are the foes. He or she must decide who to listen to.

Once the person has made it through the course, ask him or her: **How did you decide whom to listen to? How did you feel when you followed instructions that tripped you up?**

Say: **Choosing good friends is difficult. Sometimes friends let us down so hard we wonder if they even care about us. Jesus was often disappointed by His closest friends, especially toward the end of His ministry. And we can discover a lot about the way Jesus handled betrayal and deep hurt.**

(This Icebreaker was taken from the *Ideas Book, Volume 25-28,* © 1985 by Youth Specialties, Inc.)

Leader's Tip: More than one person might want to go through the obstacle course. Be aware of the time; if extending the activity will take away from the Bible study time, offer to continue the activity at the end of the small group.

 ## Opening

If the group feels like singing, sing this last verse from "O Sacred Head, Now Wounded." You can find this song in most hymnbooks. It's a solemn hymn, but appropriate for this study about Jesus' betrayal, arrest, and crucifixion.

What language shall I borrow
To thank Thee, dearest friend
For this, thy dying sorrow
Thy pity without end?
O make me thine forever
And should I fainting be,
Lord let me never, never
Outlive my love for Thee.

Here's a prayer to use or adapt for this week's study:

Heavenly Father, most of us have felt hurt when friends have let us down. How hurt Jesus must have felt when His friends ran at the time He needed them the most. Forgive us for the times we may have let You down. Thank You for Your willingness to always welcome us back. In Jesus' name. Amen.

2 Bible Study

Focus

Begin today's meeting by talking about times friends have disappointed or betrayed group members. Don't let anyone share a story that might embarrass someone in the group. This is not the time to get even with someone, but to relate to feelings of betrayal.

Ask: **What emotions do you associate with betrayal?**

Say something like this: **We're near the end of Jesus' life on earth. He had just invested the last three years of His life into His disciples. When push came to shove, they bailed out. In spite of this betrayal, all of the friendships with Jesus were reconciled—except for one. Let's take a look at how Jesus handled betrayal and everything else.**

Dig In

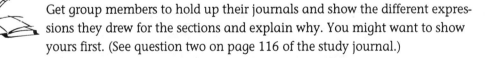

Get group members to hold up their journals and show the different expressions they drew for the sections and explain why. You might want to show yours first. (See question two on page 116 of the study journal.)

Why do you think things were so intense?

For example, things had been building up all week between Jesus and the religious leaders, and were about to explode. Jesus and the disciples had to deal with Judas Iscariot's betrayal, Jesus' certain death, as well as the disciples' fear of who knows what.

With the intense emotions of this chapter as the backdrop, look at the sections in detail. This first set of questions looks at Jesus' anointing at Bethany.

What do you think Jesus meant when He said "The poor you will always have with you"?

Here are some possible ideas. Some Christians have used this verse to say that the problem of poverty has always existed and always will exist, so the problem will never be solved. And if that's the case, why do anything about it? Actually, the opposite is probably more accurate. We should help the poor, and help them out of their rut, even though there will always be people to replace them.

Do you think the woman knew Jesus was about to die?

It could be that the woman was simply expressing her devotion to Jesus, but Jesus knew what was ahead for Him and interpreted her loving act accordingly.

Why do you think Judas Iscariot wanted to betray Jesus?

It might be a bit hard for group members to come up with motives for Judas's betrayal of Jesus. If you'd like, ask someone to look up and read aloud John 12:4-6. John gave a bit more information about Judas in his account. Also check out Luke 22:4-6.

There are a lot of different theories about why Judas wanted to betray Jesus. For example, a lot of people speculate that Judas was frustrated by Jesus' role as a suffering servant. Judas wanted a messiah who was going to deliver the Jewish people from Rome's oppression, and perhaps make all of them rich. Judas did have a tendency to embezzle. Others think that Judas agreed to turn Jesus over to His enemies in order to force Jesus into using His powers.

As a group, share some of your observations and comments about the Last Supper. For example, Jesus already knew where He and the disciples were going to eat the Passover. They reclined around the table while they ate. Jesus announced His betrayal before He gave thanks for the bread.

Jesus referred to the bread as His body, and the cup as His blood. What's the significance of these comparisons?

Chances are your discussion will center around Communion or the Lord's Supper (or the Eucharist). You might want to explain that Jesus did not want His followers to ever forget how much their salvation cost. Communion is a way for God's people to frequently be reminded of Jesus' sacrifice on their behalf.

What does Communion mean to you? This is a very personal question. Allow people a few minutes to think about this. Don't push everyone to respond.

What do you think Jesus was referring to when He said, "I will not drink again of the fruit of the vine until that day when I drink it anew in the kingdom of God" (vs. 25)? Jesus knew that this was His last night with the disciples before His death.

What do you think are the key phrases or ideas in this section?

As group members explain their choices, you might want to point out a couple of phrases: "*Abba*, Father," which expresses an especially close relationship to God. It was as if Jesus was saying, "Dearest Father, dearest Daddy." Another key phrase shows Jesus' submission to His Father: "Take this cup from me. Yet not what I will, but what you will."

Say something like this: **Remember back in Mark 10 when James and John wanted positions of honor and power? Remember Jesus' response? He said, "Can you drink the cup I drink or be baptized with the baptism I am baptized with?" (Mark 10:38). Same cup, same meaning—Jesus was about to face the divine punishment for sin.**

Why do you think Jesus asked His Father to take this cup from Him? The horror of what lay before Jesus compelled Him to ask to be excused. You might want to mention that Jesus was about to face separation from God while He bore the sins of the world on the cross. It would be like God turning His back on Himself.

Ask: **How did Jesus' reactions and emotions compare with the disciples and other characters?** Group members may want to refer to question three in the journal.

Using the chart in questions four and six (page 117 in the journal) as a basis, have group members point out different things that indicate that Jesus was in control of the events leading up to His death.

What difference does this make to you?

Get several people to share what they discovered about Jesus (see question five in the Bible study journal). Ask: **Did any of Jesus' reactions surprise you? Why or why not?**

How do you think you would have reacted if you were there when Jesus was arrested? Have group members identify with the disciples' reactions.

Why do you think the disciples bailed out, or in Peter's case, totally denied Jesus?

Here's one possible idea: It's easy to make promises when there's no pressure or heat. When Peter's life was at stake, his resolve to stay loyal melted.

What's the big difference between Peter's denial and Judas's betrayal? Peter realized what he had done and repented. Judas never was restored. Judas took his life because he may have felt that his action was unforgivable.

 ## Reflect and Respond

You might want to read Mark 14:50, "then everyone deserted him and fled," before asking these questions.

What's the downside of identifying with Jesus? Sometimes being a Christian isn't very popular at all. People put labels on you that are unfair—narrow-minded, arrogant, judgmental. Identifying with Jesus means associating with people who may not be popular—that alone can threaten your acceptance by others.

This is just a thought question—no one is expected to answer out loud. **Do you feel like you've ever let Jesus down? How did you feel once you realized what you had done? Do you now feel close to Jesus, or do you still feel far away from Him?**

This is an ideal time to talk about Jesus' forgiveness of sin—that's sort of the point of the study time. Flip back to Week 2 (page 26) for an explanation of salvation. You and other group leaders might want to talk about how you came to Christ and when you first discovered His forgiveness of sin. If other people want to share their stories about coming to Christ, let them.

Leader's Tip: If it is appropriate, you may want to have communion with your group. Read I Corinthians 11:17-32 to the group as preparation for the Lord's Supper.

3 Sharing and Prayer

■ The nard the woman poured on Jesus' feet came from a plant that grows mainly in India, in the Himalayan Mountains. It was used to anoint royalty. The alabaster jar that contained the perfume was made of a white or translucent stone that was also used for vases and statues.

■ Passover celebrates the Hebrew people's deliverance from slavery in Egypt. It commemorates the last plague that finally convinced Pharaoh to let the Hebrews go. The angel of the Lord "passed over" those Israelite homes that had the blood of a sacrificial lamb smeared on their doorposts. The festival is also called the feast of unleavened bread, because only bread made without yeast was eaten during the seven days of the festival. The Israelites were in such a hurry when they left Egypt that they didn't have time to wait for their bread to rise.

■ Based on the note from the New International Study Bible, the young man who ran without his clothes was presumably the author of this Gospel, John Mark. The lack of underwear suggests he was in a hurry to follow Jesus to the garden.

■ The Sanhedrin was the high council that governed the Jews during the first century. It was made up of Sadducees, Pharisees, the chief priests, and elders. The Roman government gave the Sanhedrin some authority, but kept them under Caesar's thumb.

Before closing, allow some time for people in the group to talk about how things are going. Follow up on ways God has answered prayers. Perhaps someone had been praying for a relationship that was broken, but is now on the mend. After everyone's had a chance to talk, lead the group in a time of prayer.

As people begin to leave, be sure to remind them to work on Mark 15 in their journals for next week.

WEEK 15 One Day to Live

Overview

• To examine Jesus' final hours before His death, and examine His followers' reaction to the good news of His resurrection.

• To give people a chance to honestly respond to Jesus' question: "Who do you say I am?"

Scripture: Mark 15 and 16

1 Getting Started

Housekeeping

Even if food hasn't been a part of your small group time, plan on snacks (yes, store-bought is fine) at this meeting—sort of as an end-of-the-fifteen-week study party.

If you haven't decided about the future of the group, this is the week to do so. After announcements, add a personal expression of your appreciation for the group, then get started.

Icebreaker

This activity is called, "Can You Top This?" Make sure everyone has a piece of paper and a pencil, and tell people to write down the hardest thing they had ever done. For example, playing a piece of music from memory in front of three hundred people; running the mile in under four minutes, thirty seconds; going without TV for a week. Give everyone a few minutes to think and write down a feat. Go around the group, and have each person tell about his or her accomplishment. When everyone has had a chance to talk, take a vote—by paper ballot—of who did the hardest thing. Tally the votes and congratulate the winner.

Say something like this: **There is a fine line between doing what is the difficult and doing the impossible. We're going to take a look at an event many people thought was absolutely, no-way, one hundred percent impossible.**

Opening

Instead of the usual opening, give people a chance to share different things they appreciated about the small group. When people have finished, here's a prayer to use or adapt:

God, there are many things in the Bible that we don't understand. Help us to never dismiss something as untrue just because we don't understand it. In Jesus' name. Amen.

2 Bible Study

Focus

To begin the Bible study, ask group members how they responded to the opening paragraph in the Bible study journal.

Let's talk about death. Suppose you only had one day to live. How would you feel about the way you had lived your life? Explain your choice.
___ No regrets
___ Too many loose ends
___ What a waste
___ Pretty insignificant

Say something like this: **It's obvious that Jesus would have checked "No regrets" about His life, being God's Son and everything. But from the way**

He spent His last day on earth, a lot of people might wonder if Jesus should have done some things differently.

 As you read Mark 15, what things stood out to you? (See question one, page 124.) For example, the only time Jesus defended Himself was when He answered Pilate's question about being the king of the Jews. And Jesus' answer probably didn't go over very well either.

Dig In

First, look at Jesus' examination before Pilate. You might want to share some of the background about Pontius Pilate in Inside Insights.

Why wouldn't the Jewish leaders put Jesus to death?

If you want to, ask someone to read Luke 23:2 for the trumped-up charges brought against Jesus—subversion, opposition to paying taxes to Caesar, and claims to be Christ, a king.

Why do you think that Pilate was amazed that Jesus refused to answer? Pilate could see how easily these charges could be refuted. None of the witnesses could agree. A few words of defense from Jesus, and He would be a free man. Jesus gave no answer, and Pilate had to convict and sentence Him.

How would you describe the atmosphere at the trial?

Why do you think Pilate made an offer to the crowd to release Jesus? Pilate knew the envy of the chief leaders—he knew he'd be sending an innocent man to His death. Perhaps Pilate thought that by appealing to the crowd, he could release Jesus at their request, and he'd be off the hook. Take a closer look at the mockery and abuse Jesus endured at the hands of the soldiers. Ask: **How did you feel when you read this section?**

Why do you think Jesus simply took all this abuse? As God, Jesus could have had a legion of angels at His side in an instant. Instead, He chose to endure the shame for the sake of those He was sent to save.

Why did Jesus feel like God had abandoned Him? Because Jesus took on the sins of the world, that is, He actually assumed our guilt (II Cor. 5:21), God could not look upon Him; Jesus' Father turned His back on His Son. Jesus felt abandoned because God did forsake Him, if only for a moment.

At this point, talk about what group members discovered about the characters and their perceptions of Jesus (see questions three and four in the Bible study journal).

Give the centurion's perspective of what happened at Jesus' crucifixion.

How do you think Jesus' followers must have felt as they watched Him die? How would you have felt if you had been there?

These next questions are about Mark 16. Say something like this: **From our vantage point, we know what's coming—Jesus' resurrection. But why didn't the disciples expect Jesus to rise from the dead?**

Here are some possible answers. After what they saw on Friday, it seemed as if there was no way that Jesus could rise from the dead. In spite of Jesus' teaching, they still didn't understand or believe that the Resurrection would really happen. Perhaps when Jesus talked about rising from the dead, the disciples thought He was just speaking figuratively.

Why were the women afraid? The events of the first Easter morning happened in a whirlwind. Even though Jesus had told His disciples what would happen, it was a lot to take in when it actually did. The women weren't sure what to think. You might want to mention that in Matthew's account, he says the women were afraid, but filled with joy (see Matthew 28:8).

Suppose you were one of the women that went to the tomb. What would you have said to Peter and the other disciples?

Wrap up this section with group members explaining their responses to question eight in the Bible study journal.

 ## Reflect and Respond

 Move into this section by asking group members how they responded to question nine in the journal. Say: **We've investigated Jesus' life, looked at the way other people responded to Him; now we have to answer Jesus' question: "Who do you say I am?"**

As group members express their thoughts, ask if anyone's view of Jesus has changed from the start of this study. Does anyone still have questions or doubts

■ Pontius Pilate was the Roman governor of Judea. He hated the Jews with a passion, and probably didn't enjoy his post. Pilate came to power around A.D. 26. At the time of Jesus' crucifixion, Pilate's standing with his Roman superiors may have been in jeopardy, which might explain why he was hesitant to deal with the complaints against Jesus.

■ The Praetorium was a type of military barracks where Jesus was taken by the Roman soldiers to be mocked. The building was located either next to Herod's palace or close to the temple. The Praetorian guard, made up of several top soldiers, were considered Pilate's bodyguards.

■ The whip that Jesus was flogged with was called a flagellum or "cat-o'-nine-tails" (a cat with nine tails or claws). It had nine strips of leather, with pieces of metal or bone tied at the end of each strand.

■ Most conservative scholars don't believe that Mark 16:9-20 was part of the original text written by Mark. The earliest manuscripts of the Gospel do not contain these verses. Church fathers Clement of Alexandria and Origen didn't seem to be aware of this longer ending (they never refered to these verses). The vocabulary and style of writing in this section is significantly different from the rest of Mark. Lastly, the content seems to be "out of character" with the way Jesus is described in the Mark 1—16:8.

about who Jesus is? Encourage people to be honest as they answer this important question.

Then lead into the Sharing and Prayer section with a time of praise, giving group members a chance to express thanks for who Jesus is and what He has done for them, especially through His death and resurrection.

3 Sharing and Prayer

After you've prayed for each other and got caught up with any answers to prayer, break out the treat you brought for this last meeting. Take a little bit of time to ask people in the group what they thought of the study as a whole—the good, the bad, and the ugly.

Leader's Tip: Self-evaluation is good for small groups, even though it may feel a little intimidating to the group leaders. Keep in mind that no group is perfect. There's always room for improvement, and that the good that has come out of the studies balances out any shortcomings.